The Actor's Workbook
How to Become a
Working Actor

The Actor's Workbook
How to Become a
Working Actor

Valorie Hubbard

Lea Tolub Brandenburg

Boston   New York   San Francisco
Mexico City   Montreal   Toronto   London   Madrid   Munich   Paris
Hong Kong   Singapore   Tokyo   Cape Town   Sydney

Acquisitions Editor: *Jeanne Zalesky*
Marketing Manager: *Suzan Czajkowski*
Production Supervisor: *Beth Houston*
Editorial Production Service: *S4Carlisle Publishing Services*
Manufacturing Buyer: *JoAnne Sweeney*
Electronic Composition: *S4Carlisle Publishing Services*
Cover Administrator: *Linda Knowles*

For related titles and support materials, visit our online catalog at www.ablongman.com.

Between the time website information is gathered and then published, it is not unusual for some sites to have closed. Also, the transcription of URLs can result in typographical errors. The publisher would appreciate notification where these errors occur so that they may be corrected in subsequent editions.

ISBN-13: 978-0-205-59231-9   ISBN-10: 0-205-59231-7

Library of Congress Cataloging-in-Publication Data

Hubbard, Valorie.
   The actor's workbook : how to become a working actor / Valorie Hubbard.
      p. cm.
   ISBN 0-205-59231-7
   1. Acting—Vocational guidance.   I. Title.
   PN2055.H79 2009
   792.02'8023—dc22   2008002639

Printed in the United States of America

10 9 8 7 6 5 4 3 2 1   12 11 10 09 08

CONTENTS

INTRODUCTION

I know what you are thinking, "Great, yet another book on the Business of Acting" or "How is this going to help my career?"

What makes this book different is that I have been practicing these principles for the last 20 years in my own career as an actress. So there is a lot of lab work available to test my theories. My career doesn't look like I imagined it would when I was 16, but I have had a career that I am proud of, and I would say 90% of the work I have gotten has been a direct result of the principles in this workbook. I have had agents throughout my career, some great, some not so great.

I went to a big acting school a million years ago. The school offered an audition class in my senior year. The class was very informative; we covered headshots and resumés, audition technique, etc. What the class did not address was how to pursue work. The assumption of the school and the teacher was that an agent would do all of the pursuing for me. That if I just found the right agent I would be FINE. What I found out was that that statement was false. It's actually common sense; an agent makes 10% and I make 90%—who should do more work? Ultimately I care more about my career than anyone else, except for maybe my parents. So—I NEED TO BE IN CHARGE. The first time I really remember learning this lesson was about 4 years out of acting school. I asked my agent to submit me for a Broadway production of Arthur Miller's *The Crucible*. My agent told me that I did not have the credits to qualify for an audition for a production of that level. So I walked over to the casting office and submitted myself for the role. I was invited to audition AND also was cast in the role. The second lesson for me was when I met a man named Jay Perry. Jay had opened a business called the Actors Information Project. It was a place where actors could go and take classes about the business of acting. I took my first class there and it changed my life. This class taught me so much of what is in this book. Of course, over the years I have added my own style and substance to the material.

I asked Lea to write this book with me, because of what she brought to the table. I knew Lea to be an actress who practices the principles in this book and in the mid-90s we formed a company called Strategies. We helped actors move forward in their careers. I have always done better when I was in a partnership. A lot of people had been bugging me to write this book and I knew if I asked Lea to join me, together we would get it done. Sometimes asking for help or for what you want can be scary, which is why it is important to have support when you do the difficult stuff. This workbook is designed to be a support for you and to help you discover specific ways to move yourself and your career forward.

DON'T GIVE UP BEFORE THE MIRACLE. Your acting career is waiting for you. Keep your head up, ask for help, and keep going, you can do it.

Valorie Hubbard

As a performer, there are many things you can't control in this business, but there are areas that you do have the power to change. Being proactive and learning how to market yourself professionally are two places you can focus your attention. Personally, as a performer, I hate waiting for the phone to ring. Yes, "hurry up and wait" is a large part of working as an actor and developing the patience to deal with the ups and downs of this business contributes to having a career with longevity. But, personally, I find it frustrating to think that there is nothing I can do to help myself create work opportunities. This book has grown out of the strategies I've used over the years to create acting work and now teach my students.

From my perspective, this workbook is designed to help you feel that you have choices in your career and to help you learn what to do when the phone isn't ringing as much as you'd like it to. It is about having a plan for yourself in the business of acting AND having a life. It is about you being in charge of your career and not having to wait for someone else to show you the magic door to success. There is no magic door or magic bullet to be an overnight success—but there are steps you can take and take consistently so that you can work and have a career.

I've had a love/hate relationship with the business side of acting for as long as I've been an actor. For me, once I made peace with the fact that acting is a business and that I was the product being sold, I started creating my own opportunities and work.

When an actor moves to New York or Los Angeles (or any place you move to work as an actor), they move to be in feature films or television or on Broadway. No one moves to either city with the idea that mailings and marketing can help create those dreams. Believe me, I still don't get excited about putting my picture and resumé in the mail or doing a meet and greet. What is on the other end of those actions is what is exciting: work as an actor. When I started thinking about myself as a product and why someone could benefit by hiring me—the phone did begin to ring.

For me, this book is about you taking your personal power back as a performer and human being. Even if you have an agent, manager, or PR person, you are still in charge of your career. They are your support team. So, why not start seeing yourself as the head of your own company . . . starting today?

And, here is one more idea for you to consider: do not give your personal power to a teacher, coach, or industry person (agent, director, etc.) by waiting for someone outside of yourself to tell you if you have talent. I'm often asked these types of questions by my students. "What do you think? Can I make it? Should I try?" I don't have a crystal ball, so I don't know what the future holds for anyone. When I am asked this, I often turn the question back on the person who asked: "What if I said no, you don't have any talent?" The response is one that starts out with the student telling me where I can "put that opinion," followed abruptly with: "I would still do it." That is your answer as well. If having an acting career is something you want, then go for it—don't wait for permission. It is your life and your career.

I wish you much joy, creativity, and fun on your journey as well.

Lea Tolub Brandenburg

The Actor's Workbook
How to Become a
Working Actor

CHAPTER

1

Getting Started as an Actor

You've taken acting classes, you've taken workshops to improve your acting skills, you've read all the great acting technique books, and you might even have a 4-year degree in acting from an accredited university—NOW WHAT? Or maybe you are thinking about becoming an actor and wondering where to begin? Or maybe you are coming to acting after having a full career in another profession? This book is designed to help you answer all these questions.

This book is a workbook, structured to help you find your path in the business of acting. You can read it through once and then come back and do the exercises or you can work through it one chapter at a time or you can use it as a resource to answer questions you'll experience as you start to look for work as an actor. You don't have to wait for the phone to ring as an actor and this book will show the steps you can take to create opportunities for work.

The Business of Acting and You

The first topic we need to discuss is the nature of the business. Take a moment and think about the phrase: the business of acting. What does the business of acting mean to you?

After you've thought about the phrase for a few moments, write out your definition here:

I believe that the business of acting is about finding recognition on a lot of theatre productions. I would like to meet with an acting agency

_____
_____
_____
_____
_____
_____
_____
_____
_____
_____
_____
_____
_____
_____
_____
_____
_____
_____
_____
_____
_____
_____
_____
_____
_____
_____
_____
_____
_____
_____
_____
_____

Did you mention lawyers? Contracts? Money? Agents? Working as an actor? Yes, these are all an important part of the definition, but the simplest and most effective way to define the business of acting is:

You Are Responsible for Your Own Career

Yes, you read that right. The business of acting is you being responsible for your own career. Not your agent. Not your manager. Not your parents. Not your third cousin twice removed who knows everything there is to know about acting but never set foot on a stage or soundstage in his/her life. YOU.

The business of acting is you being responsible for your career and not waiting for someone else to move it forward for you.

Now this can be scary and exciting. In Greek tragedy there is a theatrical convention called a "deus ex machina." Basically, one of the gods from Greek mythology comes down from the sky and resolves all the loose ends of the play. The play ends happily because an external influence outside of the dramatic structure makes everything better. This is not going to happen for you. You can live happily ever after in this industry, but you are going to have to do some work on your own behalf first.

No one is coming down from the sky to help tie up all the loose ends of your career. So, it is time to start thinking of yourself as the CEO of your own company. So, if you now own a company, in what ways will you put your "open for business" sign up in your window? How will you operate the business you own?

Something to think about as you approach the business of acting is that there is a chain of command and it would be beneficial to you to understand where you fit in the hierarchy. In the hierarchy, there are two categories—buyers and sellers. The hierarchy looks something like this:

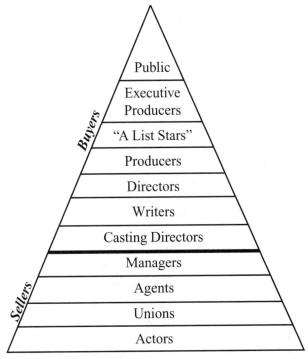

The buyers don't always line up in this order, of course, it depends on who the writer is or who the director is. For example, J. K. Rowling, the author of the Harry Potter books, definitely has more creative input than a writer who has just sold his or her first book to a movie studio. And, of course, Martin Scorsese or Steven Spielberg is higher on the list with regard to creative input and decisions. Also, in commercials the advertising agency is part of the buyer chain and in this area the client (the company selling the product and paying the bill for the commercial) generally has final input regarding production decisions. **The important thing to notice is that generally actors are at the bottom of the hierarchy and are trying to sell their services to the buyers.**

Another thing to keep in mind is that although there are clearly defined roles, most actors think of this as a ladder that they have to go up rung by rung—WRONG. If you are trying to attract the attention of an agent, the agent is also a seller of services. Wouldn't it make sense to try to cultivate relationships with directors or casting directors who are the buyers of your services and who have more control over the casting process? An agent is interested in an actor who is involved in his or her career and isn't waiting for someone else to make their career happen. So, by having created work on your own, you demonstrate your ability to be proactive.

The previous hierarchy gives you an overview of what you can expect in the industry. Do not expect to follow a linear path as you pursue acting work. Every career path is different. Each path is as unique as the person traveling the path. The actions people take to get acting work have similarities but there is no one specific way to do the business of acting. Beware of anyone that says, "This is the **ONLY** way to get work as an actor."

Here are a few examples of how some real-life actors skipped a few rungs and created auditions and work:

- An actress had an uncle who was the custodian for the office of an NYC TV casting director. In passing, he mentioned he had a niece who was an actress. Eventually she was brought in for an audition and landed a dayplayer role (one day of work) on a TV show. No agent was involved in getting her this professional gig.
- An actress fresh out of college was working at the Ritz Carlton Hotel in Chicago. She got to talking with one of the customers who she found out was in town to make a movie he had written. He wasn't just in the development phase; he was in the production phase. She mentioned she was an actress and getting new headshots and might she give him one when they were ready. He agreed. About a month later, over scrambled eggs she handed him her headshot. A week later she received a phone call from the casting director and an agent. First for the audition and then asking her to come in to do a general read and meeting. When the producer wants to see someone, both the casting director AND agent listens.

■ An actress found out that a woman she had waited tables with years ago is now a powerful casting director. The actress reached out to her in a professional manner. The casting director invited her in to audition and meet her partners. A year later, she was called in to audition for a major feature film and was cast in the role.

If you are reading this book, there is a strong likelihood you want to be a professional actor and an actor who makes a living as a performer. Before you go any further in your career or this book, **make the decision to be a professional who is both an artist AND a businessperson.** Make peace with the fact that you are a product and learn how to leverage your talent, strengths, and gifts. Decide that you won't wait for the phone to ring. Stop looking for a magic door to success. It doesn't exist. You can create your own opportunities, but you need to face the fact that you are responsible for your own career. Even high-level stars are faced with the challenge of creating their own work opportunities. Have you noticed how many "A List" Stars have production companies? Why? By having their own production companies, they can produce projects they might not have a chance to work on if they waited to be offered the roles.

Opening Your Acting Business

Once you've made the decision to put that "OPEN FOR BUSINESS" sign in your window another challenge surfaces. As you sit in your "office" you may be wondering "What do I do now? I have my open for business sign in the window and no one is offering me any parts."

You are not alone. Almost every actor we meet has the same problem. Most actors think: "I'll get an agent and have them take care of everything." WRONG—an agent or a manager are great people to have on your team (and we will discuss what a team can do for you in more detail in Chapter 5), but you are still responsible for being proactive. **Remember, the business of acting is you being responsible for your own career.** So, an agent is like a vice president in the corporation where you are the CEO. And, an agent is still a seller and you want to get to the buyers. **It is great to have an agent or manager, but you can still work professionally without one.**

And, before you start to market your product to an agent, you'll want to be clear about what makes you and your product unique. We'll be working on helping you create a clear message so that when you connect with and start to interview your "vice presidents," you'll know what you have to offer and what you are looking for in your support staff. When you are being interviewed by an agent or manager, remember that you are interviewing him or her as a potential business partner as well.

You can stand out from the crowd by being yourself. You are unique and you bring qualities that no other person has to your work as an actor and as a business person. Can you describe in one sentence that special quality that only you have? Are you clear about what only you can bring to the table as an actor? Do you know what makes you unique? What do you have to offer to this industry? You'll have a chance to work through these questions in the following chapters. This business moves quickly; rarely does someone have the time to really get to know you in the first audition or interview. What you can do to improve your chances in an interview is to come prepared to talk about what you offer that no one else can do.

Before any new business launches they have a vision. Someone has a dream. Years ago, Microsoft's Bill Gates' dream was to have a personal computer in every home. He has succeeded. And, now someone has taken that vision and expanded on it as we move into wireless technology.

So, what is your dream as an actor? What is your vision? If you really want an Oscar, go ahead and say it. If you want six national commercials running at the same time, go ahead and own it. What do you want your acting career to look like?

Take some time now and write out what you want to create in your career. There is no right or wrong answer here. There is only your dream and what you want to create in your acting career. Don't be sensible. Don't put restrictions on yourself. Do take a deep breath and give yourself permission to play and imagine what your career can look like for you:

_____

_____

_____

_____

_____

_____

_____

_____

_____

_____

_____

_____

_____

_____

_____

_____

_____

_____

_____

_____

_____

_____

_____

_____

_____

_____

_____

_____

_____

_____

_____

_____

_____

_____

_____

_____

_____

How fun was that?

You'll have other opportunities to get clear about what you want throughout this book, but here is how this exercise will help you when you are out interviewing "vice presidents" for your company. The more specific you can be about where you see your career going, the more clearly you can explain it and that will help you attract people who want to work with you. And, yes, it can be that simple. It isn't necessarily easy, but it is that simple.

Day-to-Day Operations of Your Business

As you pursue your career, a lot of people will tell you that there are "rules" for conducting your business. You'll hear how you "should" be doing things in your business. A lot of these rules evolve out of another actor's experiences in the business and they get passed down as the definitive way of operating in this business and your career. WRONG.

The most flawed and erroneous rules come from inexperienced actors who are happy to share with you what they have "heard." Here is how this one works: you are standing in line for an open-call audition in New York or LA or Chicago or anyplace, and there is an actor in front of you who has been acting for a whole year. Yes, s/he has been acting a whole year, all 12 months. S/he has done a couple of plays and maybe even a commercial and you two begin a conversation, to kill time as you wait. Because s/he believes s/he is being helpful, s/he is going to tell you "how it is." S/he might say things like:

> "You have to have an agent."
> "You can't get an agent until you are SAG."
> "It's who you know."
> "They never cast anything from these open calls."
> "Don't bother sending out cover letters, it is a waste of time."
> "You have to do theatre before you can do films."
> "Too much Shakespeare on your resumé makes you look like you can't do commercials."

S/he may have personally experienced these "rules" or heard them from other actors or even heard them from industry professionals and they have now become his or her rules, which she is now passing on to you—like a virus.

Here are three principles that we believe help build a strong foundation for working as an actor:

1. Be true to yourself and your beliefs, and trust YOUR gut.
2. Be respectful of other people.
3. Act like a professional at all times.

The rest is up for grabs. Even though there is no one specific path to take to reach success in this business, there are consistent steps and strategies you can implement throughout your career that will help you create forward momentum. Yes, this is a repeat of information you've already been introduced to, but after working with thousands of actors over the last two decades, this information cannot be repeated enough.

If you would like to set some standards for your own business, choose rules that free you and empower you, rather than limit you. For instance:

1. I will always treat people as I want to be treated.
2. I will only take parts that I am passionate about.
3. I will constantly be pushing my boundaries as an artist.

4. I will strive to get my scripts for auditions 24 hours in advance, so I can do my homework.
5. I will come to auditions prepared and ready to work and have fun.
6. I will start to pay attention to actors' stories that inspire me. (Do you know how the films *My Big Fat Greek Wedding* or *A Bronx Tale* came to be? No? Well, do some research, the stories are inspiring.)
7. I will find ways to have fun with my mailings and design materials that reflect my personality.

Maybe these aren't your type of standards or maybe they don't reflect how you want to run your business. But every business has standards, so take some time here to write down a few of your own rules and business standards. This can be an ongoing list and as you evolve in your career so will your list.

1.

2.

3.

4.

5.

6.

7.

20.

21.

22.

23.

24.

25.

Advice You Can Use in Your Business

There is nothing wrong with asking a successful actor how they got where they are, but remember there are a thousand ways to reach a destination. And, remember, what you hear is how that actor is running his or her business. You can take what is useful to you and how you want to operate, but what they do to create success for themselves is not a blueprint for you and your career. Your career will always be your own career. So, have the courage to create your own business standards and operating procedures.

Remember, there is a wide range of actors working between the beginner actor and the "A list" star. There is an entire middle class of actors whose names you don't know, but whose faces you might recognize, or actors whose faces you do recognize but don't know their names. You recognize them because they are working.

Here are a few of their stories:

From a beginning actress: "After working with the principles you'll be introduced to in this book, I learned the art of self-promotion and how to find great ways to market myself every week. I cannot begin to describe what a help this approach has been to me. Within the first month I made great contacts and was sent out for National TV commercials by various agents. Not only that, but I've started establishing relationships with some of New York's top casting directors.

I've learned after building a network of people, how to appropriately remind people that I'm available to work. I send postcards that have my photo on them and I update my contacts with the auditions and bookings I've been doing. Through one of the cards I was called in directly by a NY casting director and booked my first commercial."

From an established actor: "In terms of pursuing the business I have always attempted to approach it almost as a schizophrenic: half artist, half entrepreneur. The top priority is to work on the craft because if there's no substance then all of the sales techniques and marketing gimmicks in the world won't add up to anything.

I moved to New York and got into scene study classes and did plays in black box theatres to hone my craft. Some people go to grad school while some start a theatre company or make their own films. There is no 'correct' answer, but there needs to be a genuine pursuit of the craft above all. And then you need to sell your 'product.' This involves being organized and networking. Reading books by or about entrepreneurs can be helpful in terms of seeing rejection not as a personal affront but rather as a case where your "product" may not be what the marketplace is looking for at a particular time. Being prepared and professional when you do get a job is very important. A lot of my work over the years has been the result of someone from one job recommending me for another job or having seen some of my previous work.

Staying positive and excited about the craft while dealing with so much rejection is, in my opinion, the biggest challenge we face. And, in the beginning, unless you're independently wealthy, you need to find a day job that puts food on the table but doesn't interfere with your work and your study. It takes a tremendous amount of courage, faith, tenacity and perseverance to continue this path when things aren't going your way. And, inevitably, there WILL be times when things don't go your way but I've actually found that those are the times when I've been forced to dig deeper and learn something new about myself, my craft or my approach to the business that needed to be tweaked or looked upon with fresh eyes.

In my opinion, if one can continue to hold on to the joy that called them to this path in the first place then it's worth it because there's nothing like being paid to do what you'd gladly do for free.

The second quote was written by Matthew Del Negro. He is best known for his work as Brian Cammarata, cousin to Carmela and financial advisor to Tony, on *The Sopranos*, and Bram Howard on the final two seasons of the *West Wing*. He also works consistently in film, television, and stage.

Have a Business Plan

Most actors start out with big dreams; they pack their bags and move to New York or LA or anywhere they know there is acting work and hope for the best. Most actors give up before anything happens in their careers, because THEY DON'T HAVE A PLAN.

So, what is a plan? **A plan is a series of actions that you will take on a consistent basis to establish yourself as a working actor.** You'll learn more about designing a plan of action in Chapter 6.

When you have a plan, the detours in your acting career are annoying, but not devastating. In LA, for example, it is possible to send out 600 pictures and resumés for an introductory mailing and not get one response. Sad, but true. Without a plan, most people get up and leave town because the outcome of the mailing was supposed to be the doorway to an agent, to a career, and to overnight success. With a plan, this is just a bump in the road, not the end of the road. With a plan, the thought process is: "What's next? What's the next action that is right for me? Okay, no immediate result from that mailing, now what?"

A plan is a series of steps and strategies that create a bigger picture. Remember the kids' game, Connect the Dots? You would draw lines between a series of dots and a picture is revealed. With a plan there is always one more step you can take or one more connection you can make. Each action you take helps you connect the dots of your career.

This workbook is designed to help find ways to keep going even when success, as you've defined it, doesn't come knocking as quickly as you think it should. Other topics in this book will address how to create opportunities, how to discover what makes the services you want to sell unique, and how to help you keep going when the going gets tough.

And, if you are still looking for a linear way of approaching getting acting work, here's a formula for you:

Working in your acting business + Networking + Working on the craft of acting = PAYING WORK.

So, let's get started...

CHAPTER

2 **Branding**

In this chapter we'll begin our exploration of your product: **YOU.** Most actors initially fight the idea that they are the product being sold. One reason actors struggle with this concept is that they don't want to be "typecast." Another reason is that they don't want to objectify themselves and become a "thing." Being an actor is all about being creative and acting and not selling a service to potential buyers. Right?

Wrong. **No one can hire you or will take a chance on you if they can't figure out how to utilize your talent and how you might be a match for their casting needs.** In addition to training yourself as an actor and developing your craft, part of your job is learning what makes you stand out from the crowd and then communicating what your unique qualities are to people who can purchase your acting services.

Think about it: Would you buy a product off the shelf at the store if you had no idea what it was or what it had to offer you? Knowing what you are and what you have to offer are VERY IMPORTANT. Knowing where you might fit in the business will help you anytime you meet with an agent or potential buyer of your acting services.

Another way to think about this is an advertising term called *branding*. Advertisers create brand awareness for their product. How branding works in the marketplace shows up in this way: let's say you are in the grocery store and want to buy vanilla ice cream. Go stand in front of the freezer cases; ever notice how many brands of vanilla ice cream there are? Häagen Dazs, Ben and Jerry, Edy's, and the grocery store's brand are just a few of the types of vanilla ice cream you'll find. All of these brands are vanilla ice cream, but if you want Ben and Jerry's vanilla ice cream, no other brand of ice cream will work for you.

What makes you different than every other actor that looks like you? What are the unique things that you bring to the table that no one else does? These are tough questions and they are not about ego or bragging. These questions are about distinguishing yourself based on the things that make you unique—so that you won't be typecast. There is only one you. And, if a casting person is looking for the qualities that only you have, you will be the one that gets the gig. Of course, giving a great audition will always help you get work. Branding and developing yourself as an actor are equally important in helping you find and then land the work.

Why put the time and effort into creating a clear marketing message for yourself? When you do this type of branding work, you'll find that the auditions you do get you'll have a real shot at landing the gig because you are a perfect match for the part. You've put out a clear message of what only you can bring to the character, so you'll attract the right auditions and opportunities—work that you really have a shot at booking.

Remember, you are the CEO of your own company and you have a product (you) which you are putting on the market and selling. So, what do you have that is worth:

- $700.00 a week in Regional Theatre
- $1,500.00 a week on Broadway
- $759.00 working as a day player on a movie
- $2,634.00 working for a week on a feature film
- $2,700.00 for a co-starring role on a TV show
- $5,000.00 for a guest star booking on a TV show
- $567.00 per day for a principal role in a commercial
- $30,000.00–$40,000.00 for a commercial that runs nationally

This is a very fast business; if an agent or a manager or a casting director receives your picture and resumé in the mail and is not sure within the first 2 seconds what to do with you, they certainly don't have time to figure it out. That is your job. **The more specific message you put out there the more clear answers you will get back.** The more specific your message, the more likely you'll become known for the unique qualities only you can bring to the work.

How Do You Start to Create Your Brand?

The first step is to make a list of features. Features are words used to describe you. They are adjectives. They are the things you have to sell or give. Some examples are: funny, risky, strong, dynamic, mousy, cute, and trustworthy. Take about 5 minutes now and just write whatever comes to mind. As you write your list, also include actors that you feel you may be similar to and parts that you feel are a great match for you.

Hard-working
Giving
Nervous
Anxious
Funny
Loving
Strong
Outgoing
Kind

Then, ask around, ask your mother, father, sister, and/or best friend to give you some words that describe you and then make a list of those features. When you ask around, please don't agree or disagree with what you hear— just listen and write down what people say without commenting.

Wonderful
Kind-hearted
Funny
Special
Amazing

_____
_____
_____
_____
_____
_____
_____
_____
_____
_____
_____
_____
_____
_____
_____
_____
_____
_____
_____
_____

Once you've made your list of features, you now will make a list of benefits. Benefits are what the other person receives from you. Examples of benefits are:

- I am dependable, like a best friend.
- I always find the humor in everything. You are guaranteed to laugh when you are around me.
- I make you feel safe, like your favorite pair of pajamas.
- I make you feel like being bad.
- I'm a great listener and people end up telling me their life story.

Again come up with your own thoughts on this. Then ask around your network of family, friends, and business contacts and, make your list.

I'm reliable like an employee
I always

_____
_____
_____
_____
_____
_____
_____
_____
_____
_____
_____
_____
_____
_____
_____
_____
_____
_____

The next list is based on gender. If you are a woman, what kind of woman are you? A chick, a broad, a dame, a girl? If you are a man, what kind of man are you? A boy, a guy, a dude, a gentleman? What is the best word that fits you?

_____
_____
_____
_____
_____
_____
_____
_____
_____
_____
_____
_____
_____
_____
_____
_____
_____

_____

_____

_____

_____

_____

_____

_____

_____

_____

_____

_____

So at this point, you'll have your features, benefits, and gender list. Some of these lists you've created yourself and some of the lists you've gotten input from outside sources. The next step in this process is to ask 5 to 10 people in your life these five questions (you can do this when you are asking your network for features and benefits). The questions are:

1. What's the first thing that comes to mind when you think of me?
2. What would you say is the most interesting thing about me?
3. What do you consider my greatest strength?
4. What do you think is my greatest accomplishment?
5. What do you see in me, that I probably don't see in myself?

Again, just ask your questions to your 5 to 10 people and write down the responses. No disagreeing, no interrupting. Part of this exercise is seeing if how you see yourself is how other people see you. As you do this part of the exercise, take into account that your mom will probably have a skewed vision of you; but she may also see something that you don't.

Now go back over your lists and circle the words that you think are the best. What we mean by that is the words that are the most specific and that really resonate with you and that feel right to you. Before you cross off anything really think is what you are crossing off something that is really an incorrect perception of you or is it that you don't like this quality in yourself and don't want to market it. Don't be quick to cross things off. Ask yourself, is this really not me? Also, look for themes. Do you keep seeing "funny," for example? Is there a phrase or word you keep seeing over and over? Take notice of the recurring words or themes.

This is a good time to get a thesaurus out. For instance, if you are funny, maybe there is a better word that describes you, like hysterical, jolly, witty, or silly. Now use the space below to write those new words and include ones you circled from above:

_____

_____

_____

_____

_____

_____

_____

_____

_____

_____

_____

_____

_____

_____

_____

_____

_____

_____

_____

_____

_____

_____

_____

So, now we are going to create your marketing message. Basically your sentence structure will look this: I am a *feature, feature, gender* who *benefits.* Some examples are:

- I am a buoyant, ballsy broad who will take you through the funhouse.
- I am a playful, grungy guy who makes you chuckle.
- I am a sweet, nurturing woman who makes you feel safe.

It isn't necessary to use this sentence structure, but what is necessary is some kind of descriptive sentence, phrase or even a single word. The important thing is that when your listener hears your marketing message, s/he

GETS YOU. If you've done your work, the response will be, "Oh, I see." The person you've just shared your marketing message with will smile, nod his or her head, or something will flash in their eyes. They get you. The casting director, director, agent, or manager knows exactly what to do with you because you've put out a clear message. You know what you bring to the table that no other actor does. Rather than waiting for someone to help you fit in, you are taking control of the message you are putting out there and helping people cast you.

We're not talking about your whole career here; the point of this exercise is getting you in the door. These exercises will help articulate that thing you do better than anyone else, that thing you do in your sleep. Everyone has an opinion of you a couple of minutes after you walk through the door—so this idea of not being typecast just doesn't exist. Having an idea of what you bring to the party that no one else does will help you position yourself in a way that will help people see how to utilize you and your talents. Instead of not wanting to be typecast, which everyone is, you are being proactive and working with types that grow out of who you are (because you've taken the time to do the previous exercises) and what you want to do in this business.

Once again, branding is NOT about you making yourself fit into someone else's perception of you. What we are advocating, when you look at yourself as a product that your business offers, is that you own the individual spark that only you have and then building on those qualities when you introduce yourself to your professional community. We are advocating an organic, personalized approach to marketing and how you will position yourself in the marketplace. We advocate you taking the time to work from the inside out and you'll find that you will able to handle yourself well in any interview situation.

Are some of you thinking "Well, I want to do comedy and drama"? This branding is all fine and good, but I want to play Medea AND do Neil Simon. Great, more power to you. Well, for those of you who are still struggling with this idea of branding or seeing yourself as product, let's take some examples of celebrities who are currently working and handled this desire to do all types of work. Robert De Niro's first movie was not *Awakenings;* it was movies like *Mean Streets* and *Raging Bull*. He played tough Italian guys with boiling rage underneath. That is what he did in his sleep. That's what he does better than anyone else. Once he got in the door and had some power he was able to move around more freely and show us what else he could do. We saw a softer Robert in *Awakenings*, we saw a funny Robert in *Analyze This*, and so on.

Julia Roberts, Halle Berry, and Charlize Theron all reinvented themselves and won Oscars. When Jennifer Aniston was still on *Friends* she started cultivating a different image by doing a variety of independent films. People started to see her as more than Rachel on *Friends*. Another example of an actor who reinvented himself is, Michael Chiklis. He won the Emmy and Golden Globe for *The Shield*. Before that he was lead on a television show called *The Commish*. The character he played was a round, balding, middle-aged man, who was funny. In fact when he played *The Commish* he was a 28-year-old, playing a balding, middle-aged man. And, in between these shows and *The Shield,* one of the projects he did was a national tour of a one-man show about male/female relationships called, *Defending the Caveman*. He then went out, lost the weight, and became physically fit and tough. He reinvented himself, successfully.

Other examples of actors who reinvented themselves over the course of their careers are: Woody Harrelson and Johnny Depp. Early on in Woody Harrelson's career he played a lovable character, who wasn't the sharpest tool in the shed, on the sitcom *Cheers*. He then grew into the edgier roles he played in *Natural Born Killers* and *The People vs. Larry Flynt*. Early on in Johnny Depp's career he played an undercover cop on a television show called *21 Jump Street*. The premise of this show was young-looking members of a police force were given the assignment of working in a high school undercover. The movie *Edward Scissorhands* came later. All the great work he's done in independent films over the last two decades came later.

Yes, there are some actors who have found it harder to change their personas, people like Meg Ryan or Jim Carrey. The public likes Meg Ryan in romantic comedies and Jim Carrey being funny. But they still have the ability to draw the public and get cast in darker types of films and they continue to try to expand themselves and they are working all the time as actors.

So, if working in this business is something you aspire to, TAKE THE TIME TO DO THESE EXERCISES. Articulate what makes you unique, create a brand, and then market that—this is what it means to be the CEO of your own company. Dare to stand out from the crowd by being you.

Go ahead, take a shot at a phrase or a sentence or even just a word:

_____
_____
_____
_____
_____
_____
_____
_____
_____

_____
_____
_____
_____
_____
_____
_____
_____
_____
_____
_____
_____
_____
_____
_____
_____
_____
_____
_____
_____
_____
_____
_____
_____
_____
_____
_____
_____
_____
_____
_____

That wasn't so hard, was it? Now, this doesn't have to be the only way you market yourself during your long and productive acting career. It is, however, a place to start the selling process and the promotion of your product, you.

So, now that you have all these features, benefits, themes, and maybe even a sentence or phrase you can use—what do you with it?

You use your branding message in these ways:

1. Use it in an interview. When asked questions: How do you see yourself? Or: Tell me about yourself.

You could say: "Well, I am a buoyant, ballsy broad who will take you through the funhouse. I tend to play the blue-collar really loud woman who is in everyone's business, or the friend who is always the life of the party." Or, "I am a younger version of _____ (fill in the blank with an actor)". Or, "I am a cross between Giovanni Ribisi and Topher Grace." Using the previous example you are calling attention to the intensity of your work as an actor (Ribisi) and your "boy next door" likeability (Grace).

By being this specific, you'll be sent out on parts that are exactly right for you and that you really have a chance of booking because the casting person can actually see you in that role.

Another benefit of using this approach is that casting directors when communicating with agents regarding specific roles they are casting will often use well-known actors as an example of the type they would like to see at the auditions.

2. You can use it when thinking about your headshot and what qualities you'll want to show in your picture. Getting a shot that looks like you is only part of what's involved when getting a headshot. You want your personality to shine through in a headshot and knowing what qualities you want to highlight will help you get a shot you can actually use and you'll want to send out for potential work. We'll discuss headshots in more detail in Chapter 3.

3. You can use it in how you design your marketing materials and marketing campaigns. Even though acting is a business, you have more freedom than if you were working at a bank. The font on your resumé doesn't have to be Times New Roman. The color you select for your cover letter stationery does not have to be white. Use it in your cover letters when submitting your headshot as a way of describing yourself to a potential buyer. We'll discuss this in more detail in later chapters as well.

Once, an actress who sells "funny with heart" sent out a "pilot season emergency kit." Pilot season tends to be a really intense time in the business when demos of shows are being produced and then pitched to the networks. Pilots are done all year-round, but the majority of pilots are shot January through April in Los Angeles. This actress sent out about 15 kits filled with vitamin C, an energy bar, aspirin, alka seltzer, and a couple of other small items to people who already knew her and her work and were in a position to cast her. Two things to point out here are: (1) she sent the package to people who already knew her and was reinforcing her connection with them by sending out these kits and (2) the package reinforced what she was selling: "funny with heart". The marketing campaign was an extension of who she is and her branding approach. And, it worked; she got an audition from it.

4. Knowing the message you want to convey will help you when selecting audition materials. If you are funny, you'll pick a monologue that spotlights your particular brand of humor. If you are dark and funny—pick a monologue that has a little edge to it. If you are the girl next door, then pick a monologue that reflects that quality. Even the monologue becomes an extension of the message you want to convey to your potential employers. We'll discuss this in more detail in Chapter 4.

Another method you can use to develop a brand is to start noticing the parts that you are attracted to. Just about every actor who watches movies or great television will see a role and think to themselves: "that was my part." So what parts have you seen that have your name on them? What characters light you up at the thought of playing them in a play, movie, or commercial? What kinds of roles do you find attractive? What actor or actress is doing the type of work you want to be doing? Who has the career you want? Is there someone who is being offered the types of roles you want to play? This is one method you can use to develop a way to talk about yourself and the characters you want a chance to portray.

For example, are you interested in the roles that Kirsten Dunst plays? Then you can use this information when meeting with industry people. You say: "I'm interested in the roles Kirsten Dunst does because she has the opportunity to work in independent films like *Marie Antoinette* and mainstream movies like *Spiderman.*" These characters seem to have nothing in common, do they? If you dig a little deeper, you'll notice that on the surface both characters are self-serving and self-centered, but beneath the surface, they are conflicted and have a conscience. You can't have Kirsten Dunst's career, it is already taken, but using this type of approach helps the listener see how to cast you.

By putting out a clear, specific message to the buyers of your services you will get a clear response back. What will start to happen is that you will get auditions for roles that interest you. When you start booking jobs, you'll find that the parts are a great match for you, your type, and what interests you as an actor.

3 Tools of the Trade: What You'll Need to Start

In every working actor's toolbox you'll find: headshots, resumés, marketing materials, monologues, cover letters, and even demo reels. The purpose of these tools in your toolbox is to help you find and get work. Our intention in this chapter and the chapter that follows is to give you an idea of the tools a professional actor uses to run a successful business.

Trends in this area change frequently, so by the time you read this workbook, there will more than likely be something new to integrate into your toolbox. Investigate what's out there, but make a decision based on **what you like best.**

And, remember that you are in a creative business, so have fun when you design your marketing materials. These tools represent you and the message you want to convey to prospective employers, so it is important **that you like them** and that they reflect you in a way that you want to be known.

The tools we discuss in this chapter (headshots, resumés, and cover letters) are tools that you have to have in order to start getting work as an actor. Headshots, resumés, and cover letters are the foundation of your marketing toolbox.

Pictures

Should I have a lot of different shots? What is my headshot supposed to look like? Do I really need to pay someone to do my headshots? Can't I just use a snapshot of me? Should I do my own makeup? These are just a few of the questions we hear from students and clients.

The first thing you need to take into account when you start thinking about getting headshots is: **photographers are artists, too.** So you need to be clear about what you want in a photo before your session, so you can tell the photographer what you want, rather than giving them free reign. Without guiding a photographer, what you'll get at the end of the photo shoot is a beautiful, artistic 8×10 photo, but not one you can use as a headshot. **Your headshot is your business card and you need to look like it.**

You never want to walk in to an audition or a meeting and have the person you are meeting with look at you, look at the photo, and look at you without recognition. What you do want when you walk through the door is: "Hello, John, thanks for coming in." "Hi Sue, thanks for meeting with me." "Hi, _____, shall we get started?" **Your picture needs to look like you on a good day.**

In New York and Los Angeles you'll find a business called Reproductions. Reproductions is in the business of reproducing headshots and they normally have a copy of every major photographer's book on hand. At the time of the writing of this workbook, you could go into the New York or LA office and pick up for free a copy of a compilation of photographers' work. It is a great marketing tool for photographers and that's why it is free. Actors see a photographer's work and then schedule the photographer for a shoot based on what they see in the book.

Something else you can do is take an afternoon and go visit Reproductions, make a list of 5 to 10 photographers' work that you are attracted to, and then set up appointments to meet each one and then make your decision. You can also follow up on a referral from a friend who thinks there is a great photographer for you and your type. If you see a friend who has great shots and you like what you see, then that photographer could be an option for you as well. Bottom line: Don't just pick someone to do your photos without researching them, their work, what you like about their work, and what you want your photos to communicate. Remember, you are paying for their services, so spend your money wisely, be a savvy consumer, and get what you pay for and a photo you can use.

When you look at the sample shots:

- look at composition (how a shot is set up),
- what "types" does this photographer work with (character; young, edgy people; glamorous model types; older actors; actors of color),
- do you get a sense of the person in the shot?
- see whose work you are intuitively drawn to.

So, what do you want in a picture? You must have **a picture that looks like you and you need to be happy with the picture or pictures that you select.** There is nothing worse than going through an entire photo shoot and not having a photo you want to send out. Remember, if you don't get your picture out, no one can hire you for acting work because they don't know you exist. If you don't like your photo, you won't send it out.

Just a reminder, there are actors in the profession who aren't selling glamour and gorgeousness. So, if you fall into that category, please don't let your mother choose the photo you'll be using in your business. You do not want a shot that you can hang on your living room wall or give to your significant other. You do want a photo that will get you auditions, so you can work. Steve Buscemi, Luis Guzman, and Margo Martindale are good examples of actors who are not selling glamour and model looks, and they have thriving careers. Don't be afraid to be ugly, scary, mean, or unattractive—there is work for you. Character actors have their place in the industry as well.

Go back to the branding work from the last chapter and that will help guide you on what you need to show in your picture. Make a shopping list below of things you are looking to achieve. For instance: youth, comedy/funny, soulful, troubled, sexy, strong, etc.:

_____

_____

_____

_____

_____

_____

_____

_____

_____

_____

_____

_____

_____

_____

_____

_____

_____

_____

_____

_____

_____

_____

_____

_____

_____

_____

These are some other questions you might want to ask yourself:

1. Do you want to shoot on film or digital?
2. Do you like outside or inside pictures? What is the trend currently in your market area regarding backgrounds? (Please don't let the background you select detract from you. YOU need to be the focus of the shot, not the really cool jungle gym in the background.)
3. There used to be a trend for black and white headshots, **but color is now the standard in the industry.** So, if you are wondering whether to use a color shot or a black-and-white shot—use a color headshot. Trends change quickly, so make sure you are aware of what is being used in your market.

Also, when meeting with photographers, ask:

1. What is included for the price charged?
2. How many shots will be taken during the shoot?
3. If it is on film, how many rolls will s/he use?
4. Will there be someone to help with makeup on the day of the shoot? Be careful with makeup—remember the photo needs to look like you on a good day. Also, makeup for a photo shoot is different than street makeup. Let a professional makeup artist help you put your best self forward. Don't let a makeup artist make you look like you just walked off a fashion show's runway. If you do get a shot that makes you look glamorous and that is not what you are selling, you'll need to do your makeup like your photo every time you go to an audition. Regarding makeup for men, foundation may be needed for discolorations, razor burns, or "five o'clock shadows." Men, check with your photographer if they have foundation for you for the shoot, if not, there are several makeup counters in any large department store that have foundation especially for men. Remember to ask for makeup that can be used on camera and not for street purposes. Also, men who have bushy eyebrows, think about getting your eyebrows shaped. Unless you are trying to get Eugene Levy's parts, it would be a good idea to get your eyebrows shaped.
5. What will you get when the shoot is complete? (For example, a CD with the digital photos, two or three prints if the photographer is using film.)
6. How long will it take for you to get your final shots?
7. How many changes of clothing does the photographer suggest you bring? When doing a shoot for color headshots, think of the colors you look good in and that are appropriate for your skin type. Stay away from clothing and colors that take the viewer's focus away from your eyes.

8. How many sessions does s/he do in a day? If someone does four sessions in one day, for example, that means you won't have much time for you and your shoot. If this is the first set of headshots you are taking, do yourself a favor, set up a relaxing shoot so you'll get a photo you can use. Ask your photographer how much time do they spend with people during a shoot? Ideally, two to three hours is a good amount of time to spend in a photo shoot.

9. What are their reshoot policies? Make sure there is a clear understanding of what the reshoot policy is; if the photos turn out badly, can you do a reshoot? Remember, all you need are two to three good shots from your shoot. The rest don't need to be perfect. It is important to agree in advance what necessitates a reshoot. A photographer isn't going to give away his or her time for free—so you need to be specific about what the photographer's guidelines for are for a reshoot.

10. How do they handle retouching? An example of retouching is the removal of blemishes, shadows, or facial lines. Along with retouching, what is the photographers' policy with regard to cropping? Cropping is an adjustment of the framing/composition of the photo. For example, if you want less of your arm showing, you can have that cropped.

Another important factor to consider is: Do you feel comfortable with this person? If you don't, your photos will show that tension. You must feel at ease with your photographer or it will show up in the final product. There will be something missing. Look for a connection with the photographer.

When looking for a photographer, be a smart consumer. Interview the person you are going to be spending money with and get a product you'll be able to use in your acting business. In the last chapter, we talked about sending out a clear, specific message as to what you have to offer as a performer. Your headshot is an important way of communicating that message.

Something else to remember is that this business is about **name face recognition.** What does "name face recognition" mean? Having a dozen pictures to suit everyone's needs or that captures all your "looks" is not necessarily a good idea. Sure, you can have a comedic, dramatic, and commercial shot, but many actors are able to capture all of these qualities in ONE picture. Remember, the only difference between a "legit/theatrical shot" (one used for TV, film, and theatre) and a "commercial" shot (one used for commercials, industrial, and print work) is about availability and personality. No one wants Medea to sell their product, so your commercial shot must not be edgy, threatening, or dark in any way. For commercials, the viewer needs to be able to relate to you and your commercial shot needs to show that quality—you at your most likeable and accessible.

According to several casting directors we spoke with, on an average day for, say, a small role for the TV show *Without a Trace* a casting director might get up to 1,500 pictures and resumes for one role. A casting director can typically go through 100 pictures a minute. Basically they flip through the pictures quickly. Think about it, what makes a casting director stop and look at your picture? You don't have to pay thousands of dollars for your headshot, but cutting corners when it comes to your headshot is not a good idea. Your headshot is your business card.

Even if you have three different shots, most actors will find themselves continually drawn to the same photo. That photo can become your signature shot, the one you send out the most. If you change shots a lot, not only are you wasting a lot of money, but you are not allowing the buyers to get used to the same name and face over and over again. Most marketing books will tell you it takes up to 10 times of seeing the same ad in a magazine or on TV before we will even think about trying the product. Yet, most actors do one or two mailings and when nothing happens from the mailings they either give up or get new headshots.

Allow your name and face to become recognized. Because no one contacts you after you first send out your headshot, that doesn't mean that your photo isn't "good." The bottom line with regard to a "good" headshot is:

1. Does your picture look like you?
2. Can the viewer get a sense of you as a real person?
3. After sending out your picture does it get you auditions and/or meetings?

You won't get the answers to any of these questions by sending out your picture just once. Give it 6 months to a year before you decide you need new pictures. A good time frame to think of with regard to getting new pictures is about every two to three years. Of course, if your look changes sooner (long hair cut short, going from a beard/goatee to no facial hair, etc.), get a new set of shots. Name face recognition is simply allowing someone who can purchase your services get to know you over time. Again, over time means getting the same photo/look out to people consistently.

And, finally, MAKE SURE YOU GET ENOUGH REST before your photo shoot. If your picture is supposed to look like you on a good day, make sure you build in time for self-care prior to your shoot. Get enough sleep, drink enough water, and perhaps have a massage or facial. If you are relaxed during the photo shoot, it will show up in the shots that are taken.

Take the time to look through various headshots. After you've looked at 100 or more, you'll be able to tell which shots work and which ones don't. Shots that make you look more glamorous than you really are don't work. Having props in the photos doesn't work. Costumes don't work. "Happy" and "sad" photos don't work. Too much skin showing and/or emphasis on your body doesn't work unless you want to work as a sports model or in the adult entertainment industry. If you have a good body, don't be afraid to show the viewer your body with suitable clothing. Leave something to the viewer's imagination.

What does work: (1) a photo that gives the viewer an idea of what your personality is, (2) a photo that looks like you, and (3) a photo that invites the viewer to learn more about you.

Often students will ask: "How much should I pay for headshots?" The answer to this question depends on you and your budget. You can spend as little as $100 or as much as $1,500 for your shoot. Remember that this is just the cost of the photographer and the photo shoot. It may not include the cost of a stylist or makeup artist at your shoot. And, it definitely does not include the costs of: retouching, adding your name and border to your original shot, and the bulk reproduction of your shots. There is an old adage: "You get what you pay for." We are not advocating that you spend lots of money on your headshots, but don't try to cut costs in this area of your business—your headshot is your business card and needs to reflect a professional image. You don't have to spend $1,500, but you do have to spend enough money that you get a headshot that you like and that you'll send out for potential work.

Resumés

Resumés are attached to the back of your headshots (generally with two staples at the top). Make sure your resumé is cut to 8×10 to match your picture. There is nothing worse than a sloppy picture and resumé. If someone doesn't know you personally, your headshot and resumé are the way they make the decision whether to get to know you. Potential work opportunities are decided on the first impression your headshot and resumé make. You are a professional, so make sure your marketing materials look professional.

A resumé needs to be:

- Laid out clearly and precisely. Most resumés follow a two- or three-column format. You'll see some examples later in this section.
- Visually appealing/friendly to the reader—make sure there is plenty of "white space" on the page, think about using interesting fonts, good stationery, and even-shaded blocks in the layout of the text.

- Mention credits concisely (most impressive credits are at the top of the list to get the reader's interest). An acting resumé is not like a standard business resumé; you do not list dates on the resumé or list the information chronologically.
- Make the most of your acting experience, training, and skills WITH-OUT MISREPRESENTATION. **Don't lie on your resumé!** The professional acting community is small, even though it is worldwide. People can and will find out if you are lying on your resumé. If you mention something on your resumé you must be able to talk about it. A friend of ours held auditions in LA recently. She and her co-director found 10 people lying on their resumés. Those actors were discounted immediately.
- Cut the resumé down to fit your 8×10 headshot. Actually, trim your resumé to fit on the back of the picture, so the dimensions are 7.75" × 9.75". Remember, the dimensions of paper are 8.5×11, and your photo is 8×10. Do the math. Some people get their resumés printed on the back of their headshot. This can look professional, but there are two issues with this. The first is that sometimes the ink from the resumé bleeds off. What happens is that ink goes on someone's hands or the photo beneath yours. Your shot will be thrown away if it does this, so make sure the ink does not bleed off of your headshot/resumé if you decide to print your resumé on the back of your headshot. The other issue is that every time you have a new credit to add to your resumé, you'll have to print up new headshots/resumés and that can become a waste of money. Your performance resumé is always in a state of flux, because you are always adding a new class or a new job. A performance resumé is not a static document. You'll have many versions of your resumé over the course of your career.
- Flip the sections depending on who you are auditioning for—if you are sending in your resumé for a theatre job, put those credits at the top of the resumé. If you are auditioning for film or TV, then that section is at the top of the resumé. **Always think of your reader and showcasing the experience and skills you have for that target audience, your reader.**

Again, a performance resumé is not like a traditional work resumé. There is a format that is used in this profession that is not used in traditional resumés. Acting resumés are often divided into these categories:

- Contact info, agent if you have one, and unions at the top
- Film
- Television
- Commercials

■ Theatre
■ Industrials
■ Training and Education
■ Special Skills

Other categories that can be used are: improvisation, stand-up comedy, and representative roles for new actors. If you have performance experience, highlight this experience until you can substitute that information with traditional credits (theatre, film, commercials, etc.).

At the top of the resumé is your contact info, your agent or manager, unions, and your height and weight. If you've got a great body, then height and weight is useful information. If you aren't model gorgeous and may be considered character, then weight isn't important. Height is always important to add to your resumé, because you can't tell how tall someone is from a picture. And, if you are very overweight, then it is useful for you to mention your weight. For example, one of the mobster's wives on *The Sopranos* (Ginny Sachs) is very overweight. In fact, some of the storylines in the third or fourth season focused on her girth. In her case, the weight is important to mention and the weight got her work on this high-profile show. If you fall between gorgeous and overweight, mentioning your weight isn't necessary.

If you have a manager or agent, do not include your contact info when including their information. It is either your info or your representation. Not both.

Even if you have very little experience, there is a way of making any resumé look good. Until you have a team of people helping you in your career (agent, manager, public relations person, etc.), you are responsible for creating your own buzz.

So, how do you this?

Below you'll find a template that you can use to build your resumé.

NAME
Union Affiliations
Your Contact Info OR Agent's/Manager's Contact Info (not both)
Height/Weight? (Only if this helps you)

FILM

Name of Project	Character	Production Company and/or Director

(Add descriptive phrases to your character column. For example, lead, supporting, or featured to your film credits. A lead is obvious. It is your character's story being told in the movie. A supporting role is a character that

supports the story that is being told; but, you aren't a lead. A featured role is another way of describing extra work. Other terms used are principal *and* day player. Day player *is an industry term for someone who has one day of work on a film.)*

TELEVISION

Project	Character	Production Company, Network (ABC, HBO, etc.), Director

(Add descriptive phrases to your character column in this section as well. For television the phrases are: series lead, guest star, co-star, or featured. A series lead is someone like William Peterson on CSI. *A guest star is an actor who appears as the lead in one episode of a TV show. An example of a guest star would be Sally Field on* ER. *A* co-star *is a term used by SAG/AFTRA on television contracts. For more information on SAG or AFTRA, go to their websites:* www.sag.org *and* www.aftra.com. *Basically, a guest star's credit appears at the beginning of the show and a co-star's credit appears in the credits at the end of the show. Featured role is another way to describe extra work or nonspeaking roles.*

These phrases also apply to pilots. Pilots are demo programs that are produced in order to sell a television show to the network or cable. For soaps it is: contract role, day player, under-five, and featured. Contract roles are the main characters on soap operas. Day player means an actor has one day of work. Under-five *is a term used to describe under five lines of dialogue, and featured is the descriptive phrase for extra work or nonspeaking roles.)*

COMMERCIALS

In this section write "available upon request" or "on-camera principals for national network usage (tape upon request)."

With commercials you don't want to mention who you've worked with. Why? If you've done a commercial for a hamburger chain or a car company or a clothing manufacturer, their competitor won't want to see you in their commercial. You are generally contracted to work with a company for a year and you are paid every 13 weeks for them to keep running your commercial. This payment is called a holding fee. A holding fee is different than residuals. Contact your union for a full explanation. When the contract is up, you are available to do other commercial work. Keep a list of the commercials you've done and be prepared to share that information at your auditions when asked.

THEATRE

Project	Character	Theatre Company, Location, Name of Theatre

(In this category, you can use lead or supporting as descriptive phrases for original and unknown works. Do not put lead if you've played Juliet in "Romeo and Juliet." It is a well-known play and it is obvious who the lead characters are.)

    This section can also be divided into: New York Theatre, Regional/Stock/ University Theatre.

UNTIL YOU HAVE MORE CREDITS YOU CAN USE YOUR SCENE WORK IN THIS AREA TO ILLUSTRATE THE TYPE YOU ARE and THE ROLES YOU MIGHT BE CAST FOR. Name your scene work section: REPRESENTATIVE ROLES.

TRAINING AND EDUCATION

As a beginning actor this is where you'll have most of the information on your resumé until you start to get other credits.

Type of class/skill	Teacher	School

    Also include degrees (simply put BA or BS from University XYZ if it is not a theatre degree). If you have a theatre degree, start this section with that credit. It is useful to include a BA or master's, simply to demonstrate that you finish what you start. But, only theatre degrees should go first because of who is reading your resumé: potential employers.

SPECIAL SKILLS

Horseback riding, dialects, certified lifeguard, drums and percussion, juggling, languages you speak, instruments you play, etc. . . . MAKE SURE THAT WHAT YOU PUT IN THIS CATEGORY IS SOMETHING THAT YOU CAN DO.

    ALSO, THIS SECTION ON YOUR RESUMÉ CAN LEAD TO CON-VERSATIONS. BE PREPARED TO TALK ABOUT YOUR SKILLS (for example, "I've been riding horses since I was 12 years old" and then tell a short story about your horseback-riding experiences).

    Here is an example of a resumé that incorporates the previous information into a format you can follow and that shows you how a beginner's resumé might look. Remember, the following is only an example resumé—the credits are not real—they are simply an illustration of the format you can use and how the previous information looks in a professional format.

JOANNA SMITH
212 555 1616
joan@yahoo.com

FILM

This and That	Jonsey (featured)	Dir. Spike Lee
Cinderella Man	Fight Spectator (featured)	Dir. Ron Howard
Angels	Jane (lead)	Columbia Univ. (short)

TELEVISION

Sex and the City	Pizza Gal (co-star)	HBO
Law and Order	Stubborn Juror (co-star)	NBC
Hope and Faith	Featured	ABC

COMMERCIALS

Available upon request

REMEMBER: IF YOU HAVE NO COMMERCIALS, DON'T PUT THIS SECTION ON YOUR RESUMÉ.

THEATRE

Annie Get Your Gun	Annie	Florida Rep
The Crucible	Megan	McGill Theatre (Ohio)
Spike Heels	Theresa	Wildwood Rep (MA)

REPRESENTATIVE ROLES

A My Name is Alice   Alice

TRAINING AND EDUCATION

Michael Stuart Studios (4-week program)	Acting for film, scene study, monologues
Actors Place, NYC (1-year program)	On-camera technique, acting for film, soap opera, commercial technique
BS: U of Arkansas, Computer Science	

SPECIAL SKILLS

Horseback riding, ride and repair antique motorcycles, volleyball, basketball, fluent in Spanish and French, certified to handle firearms

If you are interested in seeing what a working actor's resumé looks like, check out Valorie's resumé at: *www.valoriehubbard.com.*

A final note on resumés is that all acting resumés are "works in progress." What this means is that you need to update your resumé each time you book acting work.

Letter Writing

Letters are much more powerful tools than people give them credit for.

Actors often wonder why add a letter when the headshot and resumé tells the whole story. Well it doesn't. A cover letter is another way for you to distinguish yourself from the crowd by inviting the reader to get to know you as a person.

A recent graduate of a West Coast school wrote several letters to film directors inviting them to see the screening of his final film. He received personal calls from Peter Weir and Sam Mendes. Although neither was able to attend the final screening, the young filmmaker developed an ongoing relationship with Peter Weir. Both of the authors of this book have received auditions based on the cover letters they included with their headshot and resumé.

Cover letters are used as a way of introducing yourself to agents, casting directors, and managers. They are also used to ask for specific auditions and as a way of updating your reader to classes and projects you've worked on recently or as a request to be considered for upcoming projects or general auditions.

Also, in a cover letter, you can mention your callbacks. You can't put your callbacks on your resumé; only bookings belong on your resumé. Every actor would prefer to book every audition s/he attends, but that doesn't happen. When you get to the callback stage you are seriously being considered for the role. Whether you get the gig or not is out of your control at that point. For example, there may be a specific look that the lead has and you don't match it or there may be a chemistry issue. The point here is that you can include your callbacks on your cover letter and what that demonstrates for the reader is that you are a working actor and that you are playing in the big league.

Cover letters can be divided into three paragraphs. Below you'll find a cover letter format you can use as a template as you write your own cover letter. The good news is once you get the cover letter written it is just a question of cutting and pasting each time you need it. The first attempt at writing a cover letter is time consuming, but after the initial writing, it is all about cutting and pasting.

First paragraph: Why are you writing?

The first paragraph states why you are contacting the reader. What is your purpose in writing? (are you writing about representation, are you interested in a specific role, are you introducing yourself to this person as a new actor, etc.). In the first paragraph also mention why you are a good match for the reader's needs. Give them an idea of your type. This is where you can use your positioning statement and descriptive adjectives.

Second paragraph: What have you been up to?

In this paragraph mention your credits, classes you've been taking, AND any callbacks of note. Remember, callbacks can be leveraged in your marketing. Even though you may have not booked the role, by mentioning your callbacks you let the reader know that there are other casting people interested in you and your work. In this paragraph you can also mention where the reader can see your work (on-air, in a movie, or the theatre).

Third paragraph: Closing and direct requests

In this paragraph you mention that you look forward to working with the reader. Mention that you will be contacting them if appropriate (looking for an agent, it is reasonable to write: "I'll be contacting you to set up an appointment." Please avoid: I "hope" to hear from you). Stay away from tentative language in your writing. This paragraph should be upbeat and make the reader aware of what the next step is as you build the relationship.

Here is a Top Ten list that can also help as you write letters:

Top Ten List for Letter Writing

1. Use a letter to break the stranger barrier; consider it an opportunity to whisper in their ear, choosing what message you want them to get.
2. Have a hook, something that piques the reader's interest. Name dropping, clever description of self, what someone has said about you, etc.
3. Try looking at it from the point of view of the reader.
4. Be clear, direct, and brief; don't make them guess why you are writing. Ask for something.
5. Double the effectiveness with another letter in 2 weeks or a follow-up phone call, or make it a three-part mailing.
6. Do your homework; acknowledge them for what they have done. Be informed as to why you want to work with them.
7. Language and tone of letter should come from a place of strength and confidence.
8. Timing: try to hit midweek with your correspondence. Most letters, postcards, or pictures arrive on Monday. Also, there is simply more mail on Monday, because there is no mail on Sundays. During the summer,

Fridays are half-days in New York City. If your correspondence hits on a Friday, generally it won't be looked at until Monday. Midweek is a good time to shoot for because the mail load seems to be less intense.

9. Define yourself. Describe what you are selling and how you can be cast. Create a verbal picture of what you bring to the table that no other actor has. Yes, your picture and resumé will help to define you and this is one more opportunity to promote yourself with style and as a professional.

10. Have fun. No actor becomes an actor to write cover letters. Just remember the cover letter is one more step toward your goals and dreams. However, if the process is really painful for you, there are companies that specialize in writing letters for actors. Backstage is one place to find out about them. In New York, The Drama Bookshop is another resource. In LA, Samuel French is the actor bookstore.

Sample Letters

Below you'll find examples of cover letters. The first one is written to a well-known actress and is a request to be her understudy.

Dear Edie—

I have never done anything quite like this before, but I thought I'd give it my best shot—
    My name is _____ and I would love to **understudy** you this summer in *Frankie and Johnny. . . .*
    First of all, it's a play that I have wanted to work on for a long time, and I was thrilled to hear it was being done in New York again. Second of all, I think you are a perfect choice to play her and I know I have so much to learn from you.
    I mean this from the bottom of my heart, you are my favorite actress on TV, for your incredible detailed work I applaud you!!! (I also always give you my SAG award vote)— that's the "butter up" part—ha ha. . . .
    Anyway I am not sending my pic and resume, but I am an accomplished actress that has worked off-b'way, regionally, TV and film, and I am signed with _____ where I can be reached. I have been described as a young Kathy Bates with red/blond hair, 5″ 2, and am 40 years old.
    I don't know if you have any say over your understudy, but I thought I'd start with you and sic my agents on the casting people.

Thanks for taking the time to read this letter and best to you and all your future endeavors.

Sincerely, _____

Below is an example of how this letter incorporates the Top Ten into the writing.

Dear Edie—

I have never done anything quite like this before, but I thought I'd give it my best shot—
(# 3 on the Top Ten list)

My name is _____ and I would love to **understudy** you this summer in *Frankie and Johnny. . . .* (**# 4 on the Top Ten list**)

First of all, it's a play that I have wanted to work on for a long time, and I was thrilled to hear it was being done in New York again. Second of all, I think you are a perfect choice to play her and I know I have so much to learn from you.

I mean this from the bottom of my heart, you are my favorite actress on TV, for your incredible detailed work I applaud you!!! (I also always give you my SAG award vote)— that's the "butter up" part—ha ha (**#6 on the Top Ten list**)

Anyway I am not sending my pic and resumé, but I am an accomplished actress that has worked off-b'way, regionally, TV and film, and I am signed with _____ where I can be reached.

I have been described as a young Kathy Bates with red/blond hair, 5" 2, and am 40 years old. (**#2 on the Top Ten list**)

I don't know if you have any say over your understudy, but I thought I'd start with you and sic my agents on the casting people.

Thanks for taking the time to read this letter and best to you and all your future endeavors.

Sincerely, _____

If you are wondering: does this type of letter work? It does. The actress received a call and was connected with the production company and she did get the audition. The letter came from a place of passion and knowledge and a place of equality, and that is probably why it got answered. The more you can write people that really do inspire you and that you know something about, the better. The more likely your letters will get answered.

Here is another example of a cover letter:

Dear Denny –

Hi, my name is Karen Garcia and I just graduated from the New York Film Academy's One Year Acting for Film Program. I am seeking representation. I have read a lot about your agency in K. Callan's *LA Agent Book*. I love the fact that you appreciate trained actors and of course also the fact that you are seeking ethnic types. I am Mexican American and am a "petite little firecracker"; at least that's the feedback I got from teachers at school. I would love an opportunity to come in and show you my reel and have a chat. I look forward to hearing from you. Enclosed is my headshot and resumé and contact information.

Thanks,

Karen

Here is an example of a cover letter written by an actress starting her commercial acting career:

Dear _____

I'm an actor looking for commercial representation and I would like to introduce myself to you. Most recently:

- I've been called in to audition for a national tampon commercial,
- a Big Lots commercial where I was to play an 18-year-old going off to college,

- and I've been cast in a Fuse Energy Drink promo,
- and most recently booked a KFC commercial.

I'm a young, upbeat, upscale type. My type can be seen working in: _____ (fill in the blank with products or types of commercials that are currently running. When you fill the blank, give the reader three examples of commercials that are currently running). In addition to these types of characters, I'm also comfortable playing neurotic, over-the-top women, like _____ (Fill in the blank with a description of this type of character. For example, the young wife who is stressing because her mother-in-law just stopped by and the house is a wreck. Using this as an example demonstrates that you can play comedy).

I've recently completed the Master Class program at the New Improv Theatre. I've spent the last year working with them in classes and performing improv at various theatres around the city. I am confident my improv skills will enhance my work as a commercial actress.

Other training that has strengthened my skills as an actress are: currently taking classes at _____ Theatre Company, graduating a One Year Acting for Film Program at _____, and taking a Shakespeare intensive at the Royal Academy of Dramatic Arts in London. I've also started taking commercial classes _____ and am in the process of looking for a solid commercial acting technique class.

I'm at the beginning of my career as a commercial actress. I would like to meet with you and audition for you. I'll be in contact with you to set up an appointment.

I look forward to meeting with you and to working with you. Warm regards,

Okay, using the above information and examples take a shot at your cover letter.

Preliminary Cover Letter

_____

_____

_____

_____

_____

_____

_____

_____

_____

_____

_____

_____

_____

_____

_____

_____

_____

_____

_____

_____

_____

_____

_____

_____

_____

_____

_____

_____

_____

_____

_____

_____

_____

_____

_____

_____

4 More Tools of the Trade: Taking It to the Next Level

Headshots, resumés, and cover letters are the foundation of marketing yourself as an actor. You have to have these tools to be considered a professional.

After you have these tools, there is another level of tools that is available to you and that you can add to your marketing arsenal. These items are not necessary to start the process of looking for work as an actor, but once you have extra money, they add another layer to what you can achieve through your marketing. Add these tools to your acting business as the need arises.

Postcards and Stationery

You don't always have to send out a picture and resumé in order to stay in touch with your industry contacts. You can also use your picture on postcards or stationery. One of the advantages of using a postcard for your mailings is that the postcard does not need to be placed in an envelope and opened by the reader. Your picture and name are easily accessible. Bottom line: A postcard is also less expensive to mail. At the time of the writing of this book, sending a picture and resumé cost 80 cents. A postcard costs 26 cents.

Postcards are generally used as upkeep. They are a way of letting the buyers know what you are up to and what progress you've made in your career. They are also ways of getting your name and face out there into the community on a consistent basis. You use postcards to let your contact list know about shows you've done, projects you've worked on, callbacks, classes that you've taken, and how you've improved your skills and craft as an actor.

Stationery is another opportunity to have your name and picture on your correspondence. By having stationery, you can send a letter without a picture and resumé attached. This too will save you money. You save money by not having to send your picture and resumé to someone who already has one and you'll save postage as well.

Postcards and stationery are where you can have a lot of fun and really use your creativity with your self-promotion. You can work with a graphic designer to create fun postcards or stationery for you; or you can also create your own marketing materials on your computer. No one becomes an actor to do mailings, although mailings are part of the process of being in the business of acting. One way to make the mailings more interesting for yourself is to have fun and be creative with the mailings you do.

One of our past clients writes this about postcards:

"When I coached with Valorie and Lea, I learned the invaluable lesson that you always have to act as your own agent/manager and self-promote your work. Val drilled this into me at a young age with the promotions she was doing. I've really had fun with this whole idea.

Agents and casting people will say 9 out of 10 times they get so much mail they don't have time to open everything and prefer to receive postcards rather than headshots from actors. I try to grab their attention with the image as well as the information. Every so often I go all out with these cards and I book jobs from sending them out. One card helped me to book a huge national/international TV commercial. When I went in for the casting director she said I'm glad you sent that card, for some reason nobody submitted you for this job and you are perfect for it."

You can also use postcards that have your photo on them as a thank-you note. Don't overlook common courtesy as a way of developing authentic relationships in the business. Many actors send thank-you notes after an audition as a way of moving a business relationship forward. It is another way to get your name and face in front of potential employers. Also, it is simple courtesy to acknowledge the fact that you, and not another actor, have been invited in to audition.

Demo Reels

A demo reel is a CD or DVD of the work you've done on film or tape. You can also pay to have work/scenes/material produced for you. According to Secret Handshake in Los Angeles, the current running time for a reel should be 3 to 3.5 minutes. There should not be just one 3-minute scene. The demo reel is a series of clips of your best work. At Secret Handshake's website you'll find more information on how to create a great demo reel (www.secrethandshake.com).

Your demo needs to start with your best work first. Your best work shows that you are believable and truthful on camera, shows your type, and reinforces your positioning statement. Just as with a resumé where you place your strongest credit first, you'll put your strongest work in at the beginning of your tape—simply because the viewer may not watch or listen to the entire tape.

For an on-camera demo reel, in the past, a still of your headshot and your name would open the reel. Then the title of the work to be seen and then the scene would follow and so on. Today, the format of a demo reel is a series of clips that move quickly and are a montage of your work. Before you spend money on creating a demo reel, find out the trends for reels in your community. Make sure if you invest money in putting together a reel it shows you at your best. Do a search on the Web of the productions houses in your community and find out what they recommend as the trends for your community. Take a class with a casting director or agent and make sure you ask, "What are the trends in our community with regard to demo reels?"

The mistake that a lot of young actors make is to rush and get a demo done before they have anything good to put on the reel. A bad demo can HURT you more than it can help. There are companies out there that will shoot a scene for you and put that on your demo. If you do use a company like this, make sure the production values are of the best quality. Remember, your reel is being compared to other reels where the actors have done professional work in television and film.

If an agent is adamant about you having a reel, you can offer to do a monologue or scene for them in their office. The point is that the agent wants to see you work, so be creative and find a way to demonstrate your talent until you have something of quality to put on a reel. You can also seek out student films so you can begin gathering tape for yourself. The big schools always have auditions listed in *Backstage*. In New York you have NYU, Columbia, and New York Film Academy. In LA you have dozens of schools including AFI, NYFA, USC, UCLA, and many more. Also, many student directors develop editing skills as they work on their own projects. One of these students could edit your material for a fee that is lower than what is charged by the production houses.

Reels are generally used by agents or managers to send to prospective buyers: casting directors, producers, writers, directors, etc. The function of the reel is to sell you for a certain project or familiarize those buyers with your work for future projects. A lot of actors feel that you need a reel to get an agent. Not true. If you are just starting out, no one expects you to have a lot of tape on yourself. However, if you have been around for awhile, it is a good idea to have a reel because if you don't, people will wonder what you're doing and why you aren't working.

The important thing is to use your own judgment and intuition when putting together your reel. You can also show your reel to someone who is willing to tell you the truth about what s/he sees. It is always a good idea to have "those" kind of people in your life. People like that need to be a part of your team. We'll discuss your team in Chapter 5.

If you are interested in voice-over work and acting for animation, you'll need a voice-over demo tape. The principles discussed in the previous paragraphs apply here—having a voice-over demo reel that is 3 minutes is considered too long. Think of sound bites when it comes to creating a voice-over demo. Voice acting has three different areas: commercials, narration/audio books, and animation. Each end user is interested in hearing how you perform for their genre. You can listen to online voice-over demo reels from a variety of agencies at *www.voicebank.net.*

Cold Calling

Mention the phrase "cold call" to an actor and the actor looks at you like you're asking him or her to jump off the nearest bridge. Why would an actor use cold calls? Isn't cold calling just for salespeople? The answer to that question is NO. Cold calling is another tool that will help you stand out from the crowd.

First and foremost, remember that the people on the other end of the phone are human beings. Human beings who are incredibly busy and are trying to make a living, just like you. Most actors don't think to cold-call because all the trade books say don't call or stop by. Cold calling should be used to ask for something specific. Do not call someone just to check in with them. "Hi, how are you today? I just wanted to check in with you." This is the quickest way to get yourself blacklisted in your professional community.

If you can, call with a specific purpose. This type of cold call is very different than the heinous "check-in" call. You cold-call to:

- ask for a face-to-face introductory meeting
- to ask for the opportunity to read for the agent, manager, casting director, or director
- follow up on a general mailing you've done
- invite industry to see your showcase or movie screening or current project being aired on television, cable, or radio
- ask to be considered for a specific role if you are an exact match for what is being cast

In sales there is a general rule of thumb that it takes seven contacts with a potential customer before they buy your product. Mailings are one way to reach this number. Cold calls are another. Since all business is about relationships, it is important to develop relationships through mailings, networking, and cold calls.

When you make cold calls it is good to have a script. A professional never goes on set or stage without rehearsing or learning his/her lines. Cold calls are just another type of performance. It is good to have a script so that when your nerves get the best you, you have something to fall back on.

It is also a good idea to work with a partner so that when you get hung up on (and you will) you have someone to share the frustration with and someone to help you keep going. It will take fear out of the experience for you when you share it with someone else. It is also a way to make the situation lighter and more fun for you. It's a cold call, not brain surgery or negotiating for world peace.

Make cold calling into a game for yourself. One way to do this is set a goal of a specific number of hang-ups. Let's say 25, for example. When you reach 25, give yourself a gift that you can look forward to when you've finished your calls. Another idea is to set a specific number of calls to be made each day or a total for the week and when you reach that magic number, you put money into an envelope (even as little as a dollar), and at the end of a few weeks, take the money and buy yourself something as a reward for making your cold calls.

Here is a Top Ten list you can use for cold calling:

1. **Know the purpose of this call.**   Why are you taking up the listener's time? What do you hope to achieve with this call? Just like good scene analysis, what's your objective here? How will you know when you've succeeded and reached your objective?

2. **Make an appointment.**   Sometimes it is easier to send a postcard or letter notifying someone you'll be contacting them. This works to your advantage because when a receptionist asks if the person you are calling is expecting your call—you can say yes, truthfully.

3. **Know the best time to call.**   For casting directors a good time to call is early morning, before they go in to that day's casting sessions. For an agent, a good time to call is before or after the lunch hour. Agents tend to set up appointments for their clients in the morning and late afternoon when they are negotiating contracts for their clients that have booked work.

   Also, be aware of the work cycles in your community. For example, in New York, Fridays during the summer, most people leave town to get out of the city. Also, many people take off during the month of August in New York. This can work to your advantage, because if you reach someone, they actually might be able to talk with you because things are slow. In LA the workday starts later, generally at 10 A.M. and you can often reach people until 6 or 6:30 P.M. Hiatus time in LA is May and June.

4. **Be informed.** For example, if you are calling about a specific project, who is in charge of casting or submitting talent for the project? If the talent agency specializes in a specific type of actor, it would be helpful to know this before you call anyone at that particular agency. For example, if the agency specializes in Hispanic actors and you are blond, blue-eyed, and from the Midwest, they aren't a good match for you as a talent agency. Don't call them. Know who you are calling, why you are calling, and how you are a match for what they need. And, before you have this information, it is appropriate to make a short cold call and find out the information you need: the name, the project, the address, the person's title, etc.

5. **Rehearse.** Practice what you want to say until it becomes natural and comfortable in your mouth.

6. **Remember to have a conversation.** Don't just blurt out your thoughts or requests; remember to have give and take during the call. If you remember to actually take a pause when you do your pitch, you may be pleasantly surprised by being invited in to meet with the person you are talking with. The point here is to build in time for the listener to respond to what you are saying.

7. **Get a buddy.** Things are more fun with a partner. A buddy can help you stay out of negativity. When you are alone and someone hangs up on you, it is a very lonely and sad moment. When someone is with you, there is another person there to help you gain perspective and help you move on—to the next call.

8. **Take names.** Even if you just get through to the receptionist and she says: "Just send in your picture and resumé and someone will look at it, *eventually*." What you say is: "Thank you. And, to whom am I speaking with?" She'll say: "Margaret" (or none of your business). So, next time you call, you can ask for Margaret or if she answers the phone again say something polite to her using her name. An actress we know heard about a production she was right for, so she called to find out whom to send her picture and resumé. The person on the other end of the line said: "Just send it to the box office. It will be looked at." The actress wanted a name and asked directly: "Who is responsible for casting decisions?" She got the name. She went through the appropriate channels

with her headshot and resumé AND wrote a personal note to the casting person mentioning her headshot and resumé were going through the appropriate channels. She got called in for the audition, got a callback, and got her Actors Equity card.

9. **Don't let last the call be a bad call.** End your day on an upbeat note. If you don't, the phone will weigh 3,000 pounds the next day.

10. **Reward yourself.** If you are not having fun doing this work, then maybe this isn't the work for you.

Acting is a difficult profession. If you aren't having fun, then all the stress you'll experience has no meaning or context. If you are having fun and remember what you are working toward, the stress becomes a little detour, not something that can knock you off the path you want to travel.

A great cold-calling resource is: *www.wendyweiss.com*. This site is targeted to people who have to make cold calls for their businesses. It has a lot of information you can use. Just remember to adapt what you read to your needs and the business of acting.

Here is an example of a script for a phone call:

RECEPTIONIST: Hello.

ACTOR: Hello. May I speak with John Doe?

RECEPTIONIST: Who's calling, please?

ACTOR: Jane Smith.

RECEPTIONIST: (with a clipped manner) And, this is in reference to. . . .

ACTOR: I sent John an invitation to the showcase I'm appearing in and I would like to know if I can make a reservation for him.

RECEPTIONIST: (dismissively) Well, if you sent the invitation through the mail, I'm sure he's seen it. He's busy at the moment.

ACTOR: Well, thank you for your time. And, may I ask who I am speaking with?

RECEPTIONIST: (considers hanging up, then) . . . I'm Molly.

ACTOR: (with sincerity) Thanks, Molly. You've been a great help. And, we'd love to have YOU come see our showcase. It is a series of comedic scenes and we are serving food and drinks and we've designed it to be a fun evening.

RECEPTIONIST: No, thank you, Jane. That's a very sweet offer. Good-bye.

Here are few things to consider as you read the above script:

- Jane Smith asks for John Doe with his actual name, rather than Mr. Doe. By using his name, rather than Mister or Missus, it makes it seem that Jane is familiar with John.
- Notice that Jane does not ask whether the office received the postcard but trusts that the post office did their job. If she had asked if the postcard had been delivered, the conversation could be shut down by a simple "no" and then she would have no other direction to take the conversation.
- She asks for the name of the person she is speaking with, so that even though she has not gotten through to John, she has now opened the door to a new relationship. Often, the person who answers the phone today is a casting director in the near future.
- She extends the invitation to the person she did manage to get through to at the office, Molly.
- And, although the conversation did not flow smoothly, Jane kept going and worked the conversation around to promoting herself and the show she is in.
- She had a great hook; her description of the show was interesting enough to get the listener's interest.

Intuition

Yes, you read that correctly. Intuition is a tool of the trade. In fact, it may be one of the best tools you have in your toolbox. One thing you can count on is that everyone in this business has an opinion. All the way from your Great Aunt Mabel to the local acting school teacher to a prospective agent you'll be working with—they all have an opinion of how you should look, what you should do in your career, and what your headshot should or shouldn't look like.

So, how do you handle this overwhelming tidal wave of information and opinions? You handle the opinions by LEARNING TO TRUST YOURSELF and your vision for your career. In each of us, there is an inner wisdom that, when invited in, can guide us. There are lots of books out there that can help you develop your intuitive intelligence. Intuition shows up differently for every person. The first step in learning how to leverage your intuition as a powerful and practical tool you can use is to simply begin to pay attention it. Intuition can show up as words, feelings, images, and symbols. Learn how your inner wisdom communicates with you. Basically, intuition is knowing what you need to know, right when you need to know it. So, when you harness your intuitive intelligence and combine it with your rational mind and emotional processes, you've got a tool you can count on in any situation. So, when information and opinions come to you at a relentless pace, you can tap into your intuition.

Another benefit in developing your intuitive muscles is that your instincts as a performer will improve. You'll be able to trust your inklings and act on them. Your instrument as a performer will become more fluid. You'll find you start to make more bold choices organically because you trust your instrument and inklings and you'll find you "go with the flow."

Intuition can work for you in this way: you attend an audition and it is unorganized, the auditors are running two hours late, and you are asked to do something uncomfortable in the audition that makes no sense to you as a performer, or you are asked to improvise dialogue (because there is no script) and you get the feeling that the director has no idea what s/he is doing—THESE ARE RED FLAGS. Why? If the audition is making you uncomfortable, it is more than likely that if you get cast, you'll find the process/project an unpleasant experience. Remember, if something walks like a duck, smells like a duck, and sounds like a duck—it probably is a duck.

Your time is important. Think about the fact that if you take this gig, you won't be available for something that does feel right to you and challenges you as a performer and/or helps you move your career forward.

Intuition is a muscle. Learn how to develop it and remember as with any muscle—it will take you time to develop and to learn to trust it. Once you've developed this muscle it is a valuable tool that will be there exactly when you need it.

Monologues

Monologues are as much a marketing tool as your headshot and resumé. They are marketing tools because they help you define your brand. Monologues are an invitation to the viewer to see what makes you unique. They are an invaluable tool because you get to choose what you want the viewer to know about you, your personality, and your performance ability. Your monologue is another way to reinforce the message you are communicating about yourself in your business and as a performer.

The industry standard is to have four monologues performance ready at any time. You need two contrasting contemporary and two contrasting classical pieces. Truthfully, not many actors have these four ready. You do need at least **two contrasting contemporary pieces,** and definitely one monologue you have fun doing. If you're not having fun doing your monologue, chances are whoever is watching won't enjoy it either.

Monologues are used to audition for classes/schools, for general introductory meetings with agents and casting directors, often for the first round of auditions for plays, and general auditions for a theatre season. Occasionally you'll be asked to bring in a monologue for a film audition; it happens, but it happens rarely.

Once again, if you are a beginning actor and don't have any tape of yourself on a demo reel, remember you can use your monologue as a way of demonstrating your talent. So, if an agent says to you, for example: "Send me your reel and then we'll talk." And, you think to yourself: "Oh, no! I have no tape!" What you can say is: "I'm in the process of putting together a reel, and in the meantime, can I set up an appointment with you to do my monologue for you? That way, you can see my work now." You may hear "no" to your request, but at least you responded like a professional and didn't let yourself get pushed around.

Two factors to consider when selecting a monologue are content and time. Time meaning that monologues should not be longer than 2 minutes. Remember, 2 minutes max. There is also a trend where monologues are now 1 minute long. You may wonder how anyone can tell if you have talent by watching a 1-minute monologue; but, remember, you are auditioning for professionals who know what to look for and can tell in the first 30 seconds of your monologue whether you have something that they are looking for.

It is important that you time your monologue. If someone asks for two 2-minute monologues (4 minutes total of performing time) and you come in with 5 minutes, you will be cut off at 4 minutes. As a performer it is really sad to not have the chance to complete the material you've prepared. Save yourself the disappointment and work within the time parameters you are given. You may want to find material that is under 2 minutes; that way you have the time to take pauses when you perform instead of rushing through the material to make sure you get all the words in under 2 minutes.

Content is another crucial factor. Look for a monologue that is "active." Many monologues are stories, reminiscences, and exposition (giving information pertinent to the storyline). These are tough monologues to perform because you are relating a past experience in the present and don't have a strong action/objective to play in the present. An appropriate monologue choice is something where you are taking an action in the present and want something from the other person. For example: "I'm breaking up with you now because. . . ," "I want to convince you to move in with me because. . . ,"

"I'm angry with you because your behavior is out of line. . . ." A monologue, even though you are the only one speaking, is still a dialogue. You want something from the other person. These make for interesting monologues.

Make sure that your monologue is age appropriate. If you are 18, don't pick a monologue that a 45-year-old would do. Why? In the professional world, you don't cast an 18-year-old to play a 45-year-old because you can actually get a real 45-year-old person to play the part that is being cast.

When selecting your material, what part of your personality are you showing? If you are selling funny, obviously a monologue that shows your ability to play comedy is the monologue that you'll use in most audition situations. If you want to portray dark, intense, dangerous characters, then select material that shows that part of you. Regarding contrasting material—if you pick material that shows your dark side, pick another monologue that shows sensitivity and likeability or an ability to play comedy. Consider selecting material from a play that you could actually be cast for. For example, if someone was casting Romeo and Juliet, and you are the right look and age for Juliet, then by all means work on her monologues for audition purposes. If you are the age of Juliet's mother, then don't work on Juliet's material. Consider looking at Lady Capulet's lines.

Remember to be aware of the environment you are auditioning in and adjust your monologue to fit the space. Years ago, an actress we know attended a general audition for a theatre's upcoming season and an audition for a specific play in the same day. The first audition was in a 600-seat house. As with any theatre actress, she is trained to make sure the audience member in the last row can hear her as well as the person in the front row. The next audition was in a small, "black box" theatre that seated less than 50 people. She forgot to adjust her performance and people walking across the street outside the theatre could hear her audition. Another actress did a general audition for a casting director. As the actress sat down to speak with the casting director, the casting director reminded her that she cast for television. Why? The actress again could be heard across the street. So, the actress immediately adjusted the size of her work to be more appropriate for television. Be aware of your environment and who you are auditioning for and what they cast.

And finally, don't pick extreme material. If you are auditioning for an agent or casting director, more than likely you'll be auditioning in an office or at the desk of the auditor. You don't want to be yelling at the top of your lungs or breaking down in tears or throwing a chair across a desk in someone's office. The viewer will not be impressed with your acting range. The thing about these types of extreme monologues is that in the context of a play or film, you have a story that leads up to this emotional climax and a storyline that will tie up the loose ends after the emotional climax. In an audition situation with a monologue, you are performing one moment in time—not the entire story. Have a beginning, middle, and end when you perform your monologue as an audition piece. Take your audience on a journey.

The Interview

The two questions you will be asked over and over in this business are:

"Can you tell me about yourself."
and
"How do you see yourself?"

Auditions are more than just you walking in, smiling, and then doing your monologue or scene. There is some small talk. As with any job interview, you'll find yourself having a conversation with your interviewer, and you can prepare for the conversation portion of your interviews/auditions. Most acting interviews include these questions at some point. So, do yourself a favor and prepare CLEAR ANSWERS FOR BOTH OF THESE QUESTIONS.

Recently, one of our students prepared these questions in class prior to graduation. Right after graduation he got an interview with a top agent. **He was asked these exact questions** and because he was prepared the interview went smoothly and he signed on with the agency. Acting as a business is more than your talent. It requires an ability to sell yourself. Remember, you are the product and you need to explain the benefits of your product to potential buyers.

Think about the answers to these questions as short monologues, and just as with any monologue, prepare and rehearse the material before you perform it. Remember to keep these answers short, sweet, and to the point. They should be around a minute long and give the listener information that they can use when casting you. The important thing is they must see you and get you and know what they can do with you in a minute. Remember, no rambling. Just as a monologue is really a dialogue, the same holds true here as well. The point of your story is to communicate with the listener. The story is not about you. The story is giving the listener information about you and how to cast you.

Here's an example of how this works. One of Val's students recently was doing a mock agent interview when she was asked the age-old question: "How do you see yourself?" She said: "Well, you know, I am the best friend type." When prodded a little further, she said: "Well, I am the best friend type, who is really nice on the outside, but troubled on the inside." BINGO. Now that is specific. As soon as you become specific with someone, they tend to get a clear image in their head. When the listener "gets" you, you'll see a physical reaction, such as their eyes will widen with recognition, they'll nod their head, or smile. There is a shared "a-ha" moment. All of a sudden they know what you are and how to cast you. Specificity is strength.

Not everyone will respond to you; not everyone "gets" you. You don't connect with everyone in your day-to-day life and the same holds true in acting. The good news is that when you share a connection with your listener that person will remember you and will eventually hire you because you've been specific and made a connection.

Another approach to "tell me about yourself" is talking about your accomplishments. Many actors will put the word "just" or "only" in front of what they've achieved. For example, "I was ONLY called back once for a pilot." "I JUST booked a commercial." "I've ONLY done extra work." "I've JUST done one student film." Placing the word "just" or "only" before your accomplishment diminishes it and makes it small. Leave the insecurities at home. Leave the failures or disappointments with your best friend. There is no room for them in the pitch. You can always make the littlest thing sound like the greatest thing in the world. That is why it is important to write down your answers to these questions, and memorize and rehearse them. We all get nervous in an interview situation and the best way to handle the nerves is to rehearse prior to the interview. You would never go on stage without rehearsing before the performance. Why would you go into an interview unprepared?

In the beginning of your career, you are responsible for creating your own buzz. So, instead of saying "I just" or "I only," rephrase your accomplishments this way: "I recently booked a great commercial where I played a funny, disgruntled office worker. I would love to book a role on a sitcom that takes place in an office." These sentences tell the listener: (1) you are a working actor, (2) the most recent role you've been cast in, (3) why being cast in this role is a perfect fit for you, and (4) puts out feelers for future work since so many sitcoms take place in an office. Just as in a scene you have subtext, your "lines" in an interview will also have subtext. The point here is that the interview is as important as the audition. You have face-to-face time with a potential employer (director, casting director, agent) so make every minute count.

So, how do you create your answers to these questions? One way is to build little stories around what you are marketing as a performer. So, for example, let's say you are selling "grungy guy who makes you chuckle." Tell stories about your high school experiences. You can talk about the trouble you got into as a kid. Mention that you and the principal were on a first name basis by the time you got out of high school. And, in college you were on the 6-year plan (instead of the traditional 4-year plan). The important thing to remember here is that you are not looking for work as the CEO of a bank. What you are trying to do is create opportunities for work as the grungy guy who makes you chuckle. So you can tell your "bad boy" stories in this context. Don't be shy; these stories will help you get work.

When someone says "tell me about yourself," remember, don't tell stories about how your little sister won a spelling bee in third grade. No one cares. What is important is that you leave behind a clear idea of who you are and how to cast you (not how to cast your little sister).

Slate and Audition/Interview Behavior

In an audition, a slate is you introducing yourself prior to giving your prepared read. So a slate is: "Hi my name is _____." And, then you smile after saying your name. Often you'll be asked for your agent, contact info, and/or the role you are reading for. In that case you say: "You can reach me at *(your contact number, including area code)*, and I am reading for the role of _____." If your agent has sent you on this audition, do not give your contact information; only give your agent's information.

The slate is also an important part of the audition. It is an opportunity for you to show your personality and how pleasant you are to work with. Think about it this way: You are about to read for the role of a serial killer, the slate gives you a chance to demonstrate what a pleasant normal person you are and shows your versatility and range because you shift quickly from one persona to another.

Your audition begins the second you walk into the building, and does not end until you walk out of the building and around the corner. A professional actor "acts" appropriately in the waiting room as well as the audition room. If you are loud and obnoxious in the waiting room or on your cell phone or rude to the assistant, you could very well blow your chances for the role before you even get into the room. Your behavior is being assessed by everyone in the waiting room. The perception is that how you act in the waiting room is how you will act on set.

You might have had a great audition, but at the end of the day when the assistant informs their boss of your behavior in the waiting room, your inappropriate behavior will come back to haunt you. Talent is only one aspect of a successful acting career; being a pleasant professional is also a crucial element in this equation. It is a small world and word will get around about your bad behavior. Even as an established actor, at some point people stop wanting to work with you.

Something that will help you remember to be professional and polite in all your business transactions is this: The assistant you are being rude to today will be a casting director tomorrow.

Your audition does not end until you leave the building and are around the corner. Why? You can blow an audition when leaving the room and commenting on your performance. For example, you think you gave a bad read, you didn't carry out any of the choices you had planned, and your timing was off. This is what YOU think. So, you roll your eyes, apologize, and leave the room in defeat. What happened in the real world, not in your head, is that the auditors liked your read and were thinking of calling you back. When you convey the message that you failed, you've just changed their minds; so there's no callback for you. Save the drama for when you are acting, not as you exit the audition room. If you feel like venting, wait until you are out of the building and around the corner.

Remember, auditions are job interviews. Not only are you being asked to demonstrate talent, the auditors are also looking at you and wondering if the director will be able to spend 16 hours on set with you.

Casting Director Workshops

Casting director workshops are controversial. They are controversial because you are paying for the privilege of meeting people in the industry. Putting controversy aside, what these workshops are is another marketing tool you can choose to use or not use. On the West Coast these types of workshops are also called Cold Reading Workshops.

How they work: you pay to meet casting directors, agents, managers, and directors. You can pay anywhere between $25–$40 to meet with and audition for an industry professional. There are no guarantees that you will get work from your meeting; that's what makes this type of marketing controversial. There are also no guarantees that your mailings or any of your other marketing activities will get you auditions. These networking opportunities are a chance for you to get face-to-face time with potential employers. You want to stand out from the crowd; this is one way to do it.

For example, you've been mailing a casting director for over a year and there has been no interest in you or any response to your mailings. So, you look through the trade papers and see where this casting director attends workshops. Schedule a meeting and you finally have the opportunity to meet with this casting director. Again, there are no guarantees you'll get work from the meeting. What you will get from your financial investment is this casting director now has a sense of you as a person rather than one of the hundreds of pictures and resumés that constantly go across their desk.

These meetings are also a way to start a relationship with potential employers. Think of these workshops/readings as one way of helping you to move closer to getting work. These types of workshops are only one method of marketing in your marketing toolbox. Don't forget your mailings, don't forget thank-you notes, and don't forget to stay in contact with your contacts. It is not necessary or useful to meet the same person when you have nothing new to report or show in the meeting. Make sure that when you contact potential buyers you use a mix of the various marketing techniques available to you. Use these workshops as only one of the tools in your marketing toolbox.

These meet and greets have a few different formats. In New York most one-on-one meetings last about 8 minutes. During these 8 minutes you'll talk about yourself (yes, there is that "tell me about yourself" question again) and you'll do your monologue. Then you are out the door. The format really depends on the industry guest and his/her preference. For example, a commercial casting director will want to hear you do commercial copy. A television casting director can have you read sides (a scene) in order to see how you do with cold reading. Sometimes you'll get to meet the industry guest privately and other times you'll be working in front of a class of people. In order to make sure you spend your money wisely, research the industry guest before you get to the meeting. If you don't want to do commercials, then don't meet an agent or casting director that specializes in commercials. It is a waste of your time and money.

In LA, the format is generally cold reading; it is not one on one. You come into the room with a group of actors and the industry guest talks about themselves for a 15-minute period. Then there is a question-and-answer period. Then the industry guest assigns scenes or commercial copy. You get 15 minutes to look over your script and then you audition in front of the whole class. You can find these types of workshops in Chicago and San Francisco as well.

Once you've met someone, don't let the ball drop. Follow through and build on the relationship you've started during the workshop. Send a thank-you note (if you made a connection and/or did a good read) and stay in contact with the person by sending updates on work you've booked or classes you've taken.

Classes are another tool you can use to market yourself. Actors take acting classes for a variety of reasons, but two primary reasons are: (1) to grow as an artist and to make mistakes and (2) to study with potential employers. Don't use the classes with industry people as a venue for making mistakes and growing as an artist. There is a time and place for this, and a class with a casting director from a major network is not the place for it. Look at your local trade papers to see who is teaching a class, do your homework and find out what they cast, and come in ready to work and to treat the class as if it were an audition. If it is a four-session class, you have four opportunities to shine in front of someone who can potentially hire you. Remember, there are no guarantees, but you can make a positive impression by doing good work and demonstrating your professionalism in the class.

Websites

When discussing the topic of websites there are two questions that most actors have: (1) Should I have a website? (2) Should I put my headshot on one of the websites that market actors?

Should you have a website? A website can be a valuable marketing tool, but it is not a necessity at this point in time in the industry. A good headshot and a solid resumé are a more effective way to spend your marketing dollars. A quality demo reel is more useful to you as a beginning actor than spending your money to create a website. In order to bring traffic to your website you need to be somewhat Web-savvy and you could use your time better using more traditional marketing tactics. Having your own website can create brand awareness (brand awareness is people knowing you and your name). It can also be a place to house your photo portfolio and clips of work you've done. A website is a tool that you use in support of marketing you've already done. For example, you meet with an agent or casting director, you have a good meeting, and then you invite them to see your website. You can post your website on your resumé, but you will still have to have a traditional headshot and resumé. That's why it isn't a necessity at this point in time. It is more about supporting the marketing materials you already have.

Should I put my headshot on one of the websites that market actors? In LA there are two reputable websites where you can post your headshot and resumé: *www.LAcasting.com* and *www.actorsaccess.com*. If you are signed with an LA agent, this is where your materials will be posted. The good news is that even if you don't have representation, you can pay to have your head-shot, resumé, and reel posted at these websites. In New York you can post your headshots on *www.actorsaccess.com* and *www.NYcasting.com*. Another reputable site to post your materials is *www.Backstage.com,* for either coast.

Many individual talent agencies have their own websites where information about clients is posted. Agencies also will e-mail pictures to potential
employers. In this case, you need to be listed with the agency in order to benefit from their website and mailings.

There are also websites that charge you $14.95 a month to post your
headshot. Just look at any of the trade papers or do a search on the Web and
you'll find lots of people who are willing to take your money and promise you
exposure. Before you spend your money at one of these sites, ask a few questions: (1) How much traffic does the website get? (The term *traffic* applies to
how many people are visiting the site.) (2) Can I submit myself from your
website? (If you see something online and want to submit, being able to
do this is a benefit.) (3) What other benefits does this website offer you?
(Can you download labels? Do they send out e-mail alerts for casting notices?)
(4) Does industry come to the site?

Before spending money on any marketing investment or class, ask
yourself: "What's in it for me?" If you take a class, what's in it for you? For
example, if you aren't getting callbacks, then a class that will help you
improve your audition skills is the payoff you'll get by spending your money
on this class. If you want to post your headshot and resumé on a site, what's in
it for you? Not only is it important to be a savvy marketer, it is important to be
a knowledgeable consumer. This business can be very expensive; spend your
money in a way that gets you results.

CHAPTER

5 Your Team

There are certain things in life that you have to do alone and being a professional actor is not one of those things. As an actor, you are now self-employed. You are the head of your own company. The hierarchy in most companies is: CEO, president, vice presidents, managers, and the people who actually do the work and deliver the product. You've also got a finance department, advertising, sales, and support staff that handle the administration and technical aspect of the business. Generally, when starting your own business, you tend to do all of the above. Sometimes when owning your own business you find yourself asking: "What hat do I wear today? Shall I prospect for business? Should I deliver on the business I've already sold? Is it time to get out and meet some new and potential customers? Or maybe I should do some filing and computer updates, since I can't find my desk. Hmmm . . . what should I do first?"

Most beginning actors are overwhelmed when first starting out in this business. No one in acting school told them how to actually get work once they've trained as performers. Yes, there are schools that do train you as an actor and give you guidance when it comes to actually getting work once you graduate. But once you have been out in the real world for a couple of years you might find that you are more ready to hear what they were trying to teach you in school.

So what is YOUR TEAM? Your team is a group of people working together toward the same goal: YOUR SUCCESS. Even though you are in business for yourself, when you need help in your business or find yourself overwhelmed, your team can give you the support you need. A good CEO will delegate tasks to his/her team. As a good CEO of your company, you need to do the same with your team.

Who is on your team? Agents, managers, casting directors, teachers, acting coaches, accountants, attorneys, hairstylists, personal trainers, business coaches, publicists, actor's unions, and supportive friends are some of the people that can be on your business team.

Agents

First, let's look at why you would want to have an agent as a member of your team:

1. An agent either looks for projects that are being cast or gets casting notices from casting directors she or he has a relationship with. The agent's job is to know what auditions are available and what types are being requested for the roles. The agent then matches the casting director's needs with the actors s/he represents.

2. An agent then submits a number of actors for a potential role. For example, the casting director is looking for a male actor 5' 60", 45–55 years old to play an upscale corporate CEO. The agent then looks through their files for actors who meet these criteria. S/he then pulls about 5 to 10 photos and sends them over to the casting director. If the agent is thorough, they do a follow-up call to the casting director selling her on the benefits of the actors that have been submitted.

3. The casting director notifies the agent which actor/s interests her and gives the agent the time, date, and location of the audition. The agent then contacts the actor with an appointment for the audition.

4. Once the actor does a stellar job at the audition and books the role, the agent negotiates the contract for the actor.

The above items are things you can expect from an agent. The agent also expects you to be active in your own career. Once you do register with an agency, that does not mean you stop your marketing efforts. When you have an agent, it means that someone else is looking out for you as YOU look for work and market yourself.

There are two types of agents: the commercial and the theatrical/legitimate agent. Commercial agents represent an actor for on-camera commercials, voice-overs, industrials, and print work. The theatrical/legit agent represents an actor for television, film, and theatre work. Franchised agencies take 10% of your earnings from work they find for you and you book (get cast). The 10% is taken out before taxes.

So, for example, if you do a Wendy's commercial and for the shoot you make $600 and then you make $6,000.00 in residuals (a residual is money that you earn each time your commercial is shown), you will receive a check minus the $60 for the shoot and then for the residuals a check minus $600.00.

The agent will take their percentage before you get your check and before taxes are taken out of the total. So, your $6,000 residual income will probably show up in your mailbox as a check in the low $4,000.00 range (after taxes and agent commission).

And, if you book print work (photos of you that are used on billboards, magazines, newspapers, signs, and CDs), your agent is entitled to 20% of the money you earn (rather than the standard 10%). **Remember, an agent does not make money until you book work.** Please be wary of any agent that asks for money upfront and makes promises to you about getting you work. Remember, there are no guarantees in this business. Do your research; check out the prospective agent with the Better Business Bureau and the actor unions. Professional talent agencies are franchised by the unions.

When acting in a commercial, remember that commercials are designed to sell and advertise specific products. You as an actor are there to convey the value of the product. In a commercial, the product is the star. The ideas of "type" and "branding" are even more important when working in the commercial field because consumers tend to respond better to types of people and situations they recognize. With recognition comes a tendency to buy the product. Some of the types you'll find in commercials are the authoritative spokesperson; nurturing, caring mother; the lazy dad; the bumbling office worker; the car guy; the hard, no-nonsense boss; and more. The best way to find out what types of characters are working and the current trends in the advertising industry is to watch TV. If you are interested in commercials, make sure you take the time to watch the commercials that air during big network events like the Super Bowl and the Academy Awards. Because of the potential number of people that will be watching these events, these are a great way to learn about the current trends in advertising.

If you want to work commercially, a commercial agent is a very important part of this equation. Commercials are a fast business and an agent can help you get work. With commercials, it is very much a "numbers game"; the more you go out and audition, the more you will book. Quantity of auditions is the issue here and an agent can help you get the number of auditions you need.

So, take some time now and make a list of the type of characters you could play in a commercial and the types of situations those characters would find themselves in. This advance work will help when meeting with a commercial agent and you hear: "Tell me about yourself."

We'll start you out:

I really identify with the high school girl stressing about an important date because I've got a huge pimple on the tip of my nose.

I see myself as the loving husband who is in a quandary because I can't remember when my wife's birthday is and I need to find a way to remember the important dates, or she'll divorce me.

I really relate to the concerned housewife who has had it with her toilet brush. I'm upset because it smells and I have to use the garden hose to wash it off. On top of that my in-laws just called and are coming over in the next 20 minutes and I need to do something quick! Help me.

Okay, your turn:

_____

_____

_____

_____

_____

_____

_____

_____

_____

_____

_____

_____

_____

_____

_____

_____

_____

_____

_____

_____

_____

_____

_____

_____

_____

_____

_____

_____

_____

_____

_____

_____

_____

_____

_____

If you want to work in television, film, and theatre, a theatrical/legit agent is helpful. On the West Coast this type of agent is called a theatrical agent and on the East Coast this type of agent is called a legit agent (which is short for legitimate). Remember, as you've read before in this book, you CAN work in the legit arena and move forward in your career without an agent. In fact, many actors we know have done several big projects before they found their agents. For example, in the *Hollywood Reporter* you'll find a section called "Rep Sheet" and it is a column dedicated to what actor recently "inked" with what agent. Often you'll see actors on this sheet who've recently done a big movie and only now signed with a big agency.

Again, remember that all business is about relationships. Here is a story for you to think about: One actress we know booked her first two major movies and a guest star on a TV show, because she had built a relationship with the director of these projects through consistent marketing. Only after doing two movies and the guest star did she finally get an agent. Agents, like you, are trying to make a living in their profession. When an agent meets with you they are looking to see if you have the potential to make them money and to help them pay their monthly mortgage payment. It may take you time to find a good agent because it will take you time to build your resumé and your relationships in this business. Work and relationships provide a foundation for you to demonstrate to a prospective agent you can be a potential source of income for both yourself and for him/her.

There are no rules in this business, no magic door you can walk through that will help you find an agent, so there is no reason you can't start window shopping right now for an agent. Do your homework and be prepared when opportunity comes knocking on your door. Get to know who is out there and who you would like to work with. If you are living in New York or Los Angeles, K. Callan has written two great books called *The LA Agent Book* and *The New York Agent Book*. They are up to date (they are revised every couple of years) and can help you find out what agents are looking for and what types of people the agencies specialize in. Callan breaks down each agency and interviews them, tells you a bit about their background and who some of their clients are, and has several interviews in the book with several of the agents. You can read her book and begin to make choices. Another great source of information is called the *Ross Reports*. This is a directory with names and addresses of industry contacts on the East and West Coast and lists names and contacts of agencies throughout the United States.

All the actor's unions have offices in major cities around the United States. The local union offices have listings of all the franchised agents in your area. If you aren't a union member, get to know an actor who is a member of the unions and ask him/her to help you get a copy of the list. Being an actor is sometimes like being a detective. Ask other actor's, listen to other actors, and do research on the Web. Call your local union headquarters, even if you are not yet a member, and ask, ask, ask. If you don't ask you will never know.

Now make a list of agents that you would like to work with. If the only agent you have ever heard of is William Morris, and you would like to work with them, write it down, it's a start. But then go out there and do some research on other agencies and keep this ongoing list for yourself:

_____

_____

_____

_____

_____

_____

_____

_____

_____

_____

_____

_____

_____

_____

_____

_____

_____

_____

_____

_____

_____

_____

_____

_____

_____

_____

_____

_____

_____

_____

_____

_____

_____

_____

_____

There are all sizes of agencies—the really big guns are William Morris, CAA, Endeavor, and ICM—but there are also hundreds of smaller very powerful agencies, where an actor will get more personalized attention, and even smaller agencies that are often referred to as "boutique agencies." Remember, you are the CEO of your own company and these are your decisions to make. Just be sure you make a decision based on research and personal choice.

So now that you have your list of agencies, now what? Go back to Chapter 4 and the letter writing section. Write a letter to each of the agents/agencies on your list. It is important to introduce yourself, tell them a little about yourself, and ask for an interview. Don't forget to include your headshot/resumé.

All agents are looking for the "next big thing." Agents do look for new talent to represent, so get out there and introduce yourself. Please don't be disappointed when no one calls you after your first mailing. Remember, it can take up to seven contacts (or more) with a potential buyer before you make a sale. So, you made contact once, start planning a way to make your second contact, and if necessary your third, and fourth, and so on. Consistency with your mailings and follow through will help you get an agent.

Letter writing is not the only way to introduce you and/or get an agent. Other ways you can get an agent are: having a referral from a friend or another industry professional (casting director, director, etc.), having an agent see you perform (in a showcase, play, TV show, film, etc.), or classes offered where an agent is a special guest of the class and marketing seminars.

One of the drawbacks to the big marketing seminars is that you'll be competing to get face-to-face time with one or two agents. For example, _Backstage_ offers something called Actorfest once a year on the East and

West Coasts. Agents, casting directors and other industry professionals are featured speakers at panel discussions. This is an opportunity for you to meet the industry professionals at this conference; the only drawback is that you and every other actor are trying to meet the same person at the same time. One agent and a swarm of actors. So, if you do a large-scale marketing seminar, conference, or panel, make sure that part of the entrance fee that you pay also gives you guaranteed specific amount of time one-on-one time with one or more of the agents. There are workshops offered where you pay a fee and are promised you'll meet an agent. Once again, do the math. If there are 600 actors in the auditorium with you, how much time will you have with the agent? Yes, you've met the agent, so you received what you were promised. But think, will you get a real return on your financial investment in this situation?

Backstage's Actorfest may or may not lead to future business relationships for you, but it is a great place to start your research. You hear an agent speak on a panel and are inspired by what you hear. Great. The agent now goes on your wish list and you write a letter/note saying how much you enjoyed hearing them speak (and reference where you heard them speak). Then follow up this lovely note with your headshot and resumé. You are now in the process of developing a potential working relationship with an agent.

Again, there is no one way to get an agent. Be wary of anyone who says: "This is the way to do it." What works for someone else, just may not work for you. The point is to do something. Start the research, start the wish list, and learn about who specializes in your "type." Do something and don't wait to be "discovered" by an agent. Don't assume that because you write one letter introducing yourself to an agent, you'll get a phone call immediately after she/he has received your headshot and resumé.

So, best case scenario, you send out your headshot and resumé and you get a call. YEAH! Now what? First, remember to breathe. Then, return the call and set up the appointment, and then prepare for the appointment. Prepare a great answer to "tell me about yourself" and rehearse it so that it can come out of your mouth believably as if you were saying your lines for the first time. Have a way of talking about yourself that helps the agent to see how to cast you. Prepare a list of actors that you are attracted to and can realistically do the types of roles these actors do. Prepare a list of the types of roles that attract you and why. Be familiar with where you want your career to grow. A person who has goals and vision about their career is more attractive because they have focus.

Also, be prepared with a list of people whom you've already met in the business and/or know you and your work. If you don't know anyone, then make a list of people you'd like to get to know because they are doing work that you want to be doing. Here's an example of how this works: you have a favorite show on TV and you would love to appear on the show. The casting director of this show goes on the list of people you want to meet. This will also tell your potential agent that you do your research and homework and have a knowledge of the business. This makes you attractive because no agent wants to carry around dead weight. Your agent is your business partner. You need to bring something to the table, just as an agent brings their belief in you and their business relationships to your potential partnership.

Think about what you want in an agent. Remember, even though you are being interviewed, you need to interview the agent. Is this someone you can see yourself working with?

You may prepare all of the above and discuss only one small portion of what you've prepared or not any of what you've prepared in the first meeting. This preparation is important no matter what the outcome is in the first meeting, because it will help you feel confident in meeting the agent. You'll be prepared. As with any job interview, prospective employers like to know that you know what their company is about and what you can bring to their company.

Even if the interview lasts 10 minutes, make sure to ask your prospective agent what the next step is for the two of you. For example: Would the agent like you to drop off more headshots and resumés? Would the agent like to work with you? How would s/he like to structure this working relationship? Will you be getting auditions? Can you put the agency's name on your resumé as your representation? How does this agent like his/her actors to stay in contact with them (postcards, weekly phone calls, e-mail, etc.)?

The issue here is that many new actors come out of an initial meeting with an agent with no idea of how to proceed with the agent and/or whether the agent even wants to work with you or not. Make sure you know what the next steps are, if any, with your prospective agent. It could be something as simple as contact the agent in 6 weeks to set up another appointment. **Come out of the meeting with a clear understanding of what's next.**

Managers

Managers manage an actor's career. Which comes first, the manager or the agent? Just as with everything else in this business, there is no hard and fast rule as to what is the "right" order on who comes first. There are some actor's who work for years with just an agency and never have a manager and there are some actors who only have a manager and there are many actors who have both. Once again, there is no one specific road to representation and work.

Typically, managers have smaller client lists and because of this they are able to pay more attention to their clients. A manager, as part of your business team, can manage anything from what you wear to an audition, to the work you do at an audition, to the path your career will take over the next 10 years. As we said there are also many boutique agencies that have small client lists that function in the exact same way. Bottom line: When starting out it is important to find someone who can help you get auditions and move your career forward. This "someone" can be an agent or a manager.

Managers are more difficult to connect with than agents. It can be a challenge to find the names and information for really good managers. Why? Managers, unlike agents, are not regulated by the performance unions (SAG, AFTRA, AEA); thus, the information is not as readily accessible as the listings you'll find for the talent agencies. One of the best ways to find the name of reputable and/or powerful managers is to read the trades (*Hollywood Reporter* or *Variety* for example). In the trades, when an actor is mentioned, most of the time the actors' representation will also be discussed. Write those names down to start your manager wish list.

Remember, all business is about relationships. A manager is useful to you and your career based on his/her relationships in the industry. Generally a manager takes 10 to 15% of what you earn. Recently, a student was approached by a manager who wanted 25%. Unlike the agents, managers are not regulated by the performance unions. They can ask for whatever they want. In this case, the manager asking for 25% was going to function as the agent and manager for this actor. The fee makes sense if this manager was going to actually fulfill the promise of being an agent and manager, but the reality of this particular scenario is that this manager just does not have the leverage and relationships to get the auditions that merit a 25% fee. Don't let the excitement of having someone in the industry be interested in you and wanting to rep you overpower the reality of what you are actually going to get for your financial investment.

A general guideline for you is this: agents take 10% of your earnings and managers take 10 to 15%. If you aren't earning anything, then 20–25% of zero is still zero. If you are going to pay these fees, then get something for your money. What can you get for your money? How about: general meetings, auditions, business relationships that the agent or manager can build on for you, or a career path designed specifically for you.

Acting Coaches

It is a good idea to have at least two to three acting coaches you are comfortable working with. Why? No one coach is going to meet all the needs you have in your acting career. For example, you have an audition, and you call your favorite coach and s/he is not available. What will you do then? Move on to the next coach on your list. That is why it is good to have two or three people you like working with. Another reason to have two to three coaches you work with is that certain acting coaches specialize in different areas. So, if you want to work on audition skills, commercial skills, new monologues, Shakespeare, or comedy there are coaches that specialize in all these areas and more.

There are a number of ways to find coaches. If you are in an acting class and really connect with the teacher, find out if that teacher coaches privately. Another way is word of mouth from your actor friends. Acting coaches also advertise in the trades. People who have written acting books also tend to coach or teach. There are also guide books in the theatrical bookshops with listings of coaches. Again, don't wait until you really need a coach for a big audition to find a coach. Get to know some coaches prior to actually having the need for a coach. It is good business to invest in yourself and your instrument as an actor. Find some coaches you enjoy working with and who enjoy working with you. Coaching is a very personalized thing. Not every coach is a good match for you. Once again, collect the data. Make a list:

_____

_____

_____

_____

_____

_____

_____

_____

_____

_____

_____

_____

_____

_____

_____

_____

_____

_____

_____

_____

_____

_____

_____

_____

_____

_____

_____

_____

_____

_____

_____

_____

_____

_____

_____

_____

_____

_____

Attorneys and Accountants

It is always a good idea no matter what profession you are in to have at least the name of one good attorney. You never know when you will need one. If you are just starting out, it is more than likely you don't need an attorney. That said, it is important to still know an attorney you can trust when you do need one. There is nothing worse than having the need for a professional (like a lawyer) when you really need help (like negotiating contract) and then trying to find somebody to help you while you are stressed about how to handle the situation (contract). Until you do need an attorney, make sure you read everything, including the fine print, before you sign a contract. Even with an attorney, it is still a good idea to read contracts before you sign them.

How do you find a reputable entertainment lawyer? You can start by looking in the Yellow Pages. Remember, it is up to you to interview your potential attorney. You can also go to the trades to see what lawyers are advertising there.

Word of mouth is also another place to collect names. If your family or friends have a lawyer, ask if the family lawyer can recommend an entertainment lawyer. If a lawyer offers a free consultation, then by all means take it. You need to see if this is someone you want to work with and that you trust and a face-to-face meeting can help you in your decision-making process.

An attorney can help you negotiate contracts, and at some point in your acting career, you will be negotiating. Go to a professional negotiator to help you get a good deal and do yourself a favor and find the professional before you need to make the deal.

Accountants, unlike an attorney, are professionals you can add to your team immediately. When you start working as an actor you, as a small business owner, are eligible for specific deductions on your yearly taxes. For example, some items you can claim on your taxes are: clothes, makeup, scripts, acting classes, union dues, theatre tickets, books, and/or taxis to auditions. Having an accountant who is aware of the specific deductions an actor can take on their taxes is important and not every accountant is aware of the types of things an actor can deduct. You are in business for yourself, so you can take various deductions. Please, speak with a tax professional before you start to get creative with your deductions and the IRS.

Actors Equity Association offers free tax preparation to their members every year. This is one way of meeting an accountant who is used to working with actors. Also, during tax season, hundreds of accountants advertise in Backstage. And, of course, tap into your acting network and find out if someone can recommend an accountant. As with an attorney, don't wait until you need an accountant (for example, on April 15th) before you start to look for an accountant. The more information you can gather the better prepared you will be to run your own company.

Below you'll find space to start recording names, numbers, and information on potential attorneys and accountants.

_____

_____
_____
_____
_____
_____
_____
_____
_____
_____
_____

_____
_____
_____
_____
_____
_____
_____
_____
_____
_____
_____
_____
_____
_____
_____
_____
_____
_____
_____
_____
_____
_____
_____
_____
_____

Business Coaches

Just as it is important to have acting coaches on your team, a business coach also serves an important function. The whole process of marketing can get lonely and tedious. A business coach supports you in your process by holding you accountable to the goals you set for yourself and also guides you in creating goals that reflect your true interests in this industry. For example, new actors are often told they should do theatre in order to get experience for film work. If your true passion as an actor is working in film, why devote any time to working in theatre. If working in theatre simply doesn't light you up as an artist, why focus any marketing in that direction? A business coach will help you create strategies that are in alignment with your true career goals. Instead of following "good ideas" and advice from nonprofessionals, you'll create action plans that reflect what you really want to create in your career.

A business coach's job is to help you keep moving forward. The process of marketing and being in business for yourself is draining. The business can also be hard and scary because of the constant rejection an actor experiences. There is often confusion as to what the next logical step is to get auditions and work. There is also the temptation to shut down because no one is responding to your mailings. A business coach can help you handle many of the ups and downs of your career. A business coach is your personal cheerleader.

Chemistry is an important element when interviewing business coaches. A coach is not your mother or best friend. A business coach is a professional who understands the industry and human nature. Some people prefer a gentle approach when working with a mentor and other people prefer someone who is constantly giving constructive criticism on ways to improve. You need to decide what works best for you before shopping for your business coach. Think about times in your life when you successfully reached a goal you set for yourself. Look at the events that contributed to your success and then find a coach who can help you replicate those action steps. Fees range from $100 to $350 an hour. As with any other business service provider, be very clear about what you get for your financial investment.

Another way to create the accountability a business coach can give you is by starting your own marketing/support group. Some actors simply don't have the discretionary income to invest in having a Business Coach. So, what you can do is get together a group of friends that are supportive (not competitive with you), and set up a weekly or bimonthly meeting where you tell each other the goals you've set, the actions you've taken, the outcomes you've achieved, and any places you find yourself blocked.

If you are interested in finding a coach to work with, you can check out these websites: *www.coachfederation.org* and *www.findacoach.com*.

When you do a search for a coach, make sure that you find a coach who specializes in working with creative people and actors. You need support from someone who understands the specific challenges that an actor faces.

Hairstylists, Makeup Artists, Massage Therapists, etc.

As well as being an artist, you as an actor are a product, and your product requires specific packaging for what you are selling. You have an image to project. For example, even if you are selling unattractive, having the right haircut that reinforces this image is important. If you are selling glamorous, this too requires consistent maintenance in hair, makeup, and clothes.

Another important factor to think about is what colors look good on you on camera. Generally, most auditions are held in rooms with white walls and ugly overhead lighting. Wearing white to the audition is just not smart. White creates "ghosts" on camera and what will happen is that your head looks like it is floating on a white background. A stylist can help you learn what colors work for you and your complexion. Also, makeup for the camera is different than street makeup or makeup for the stage. It is a wise investment to hire a makeup artist to teach you how to do your makeup for the camera so that you look your best.

The important thing here, whether you work with a stylist or makeup artist, is that you get yourself on camera and make an honest assessment of how you look on camera. Generally everyone initially hates how they look on camera, but it is important to find out what works best for you. This knowledge can only help you as you travel your career path. Packaging of a product is an important component in helping to make sales. Sales in this case are you getting acting jobs.

A good massage therapist is another useful team member. Why? Part of looking good on camera is being relaxed and massage can help you achieve this goal. Carrying tension around in your body is a block that hinders you from being your best self on camera. A little pampering goes a long way in helping you feel more confident.

Working as an actor is being part of a collaborative process. Your business will be more fun if it is collaborative as well. You can and will get lonely as you pursue your acting goals—your team can give you the support you need to make it through the difficult times.

6 Goal Setting: The Plan

Now that we have covered the business, tools, your team, and helped you build a foundation for your acting business, it's time to create **THE PLAN.** The Plan is YOUR PLAN and a roadmap for your acting career.

This is where most actors fall short; they don't start off with a plan. They don't think about the steps they'll need to take to reach their goals. Usually the thought is, "Well, I've always wanted to work as an actor. So, I'll go to LA or NY and be a star." They get to LA or New York, they gear up, do one mailing, nothing happens or happens fast enough, and they give up. Even if you aren't planning on moving to New York or LA, know that having a plan for the market you are living in will ultimately help you get acting work. In fact, any of the principles that are introduced to you in this book can be applied to any city in the United States.

The Plan

The plan is a series of actions that you will take on a consistent basis to establish yourself as a working actor in whatever city you live in. When you hit speed bumps in your career, and you will, or are confused as to what to do next to get work, you can refer back to THE PLAN and the actions steps that you are going to create in this chapter. In this chapter you'll also be introduced to various brainstorming activities that will help you develop specific steps to take toward your goals.

Most actors also fail to recognize that each person's career plan is as unique as the individual who puts the plan into action. There is no one certain way to create success in your career. There is no magic door to success. No "one size fits all" in terms of planning for your career.

So, the first place to start is with the question **WHAT DO YOU WANT? WHAT DO YOU REALLY, REALLY, REALLY WANT IN**

YOUR ACTING CAREER? (Not what your mother or your teacher or your best friend wants for you—what do YOU want?)

 If we could wave a magic wand over your head what would you wish for?

- Your own sitcom?
- A starring role in a movie?
- Six national commercials?
- Your own cop/detective show?
- The lead in a Broadway show?
- An action movie where you get to beat up on all the bad guys?
- What kind of acting work, would you really, really, like to do?

 The purpose of this exercise is **NOT** to be sensible. This is about dreams and what lights you up as an artist. What would you like to do if money, time, and being sensible weren't part of the equation? Let's start there.

 Use the following space to write down what you want. Remember, this is about what you really want—not what you think you should do in order to get to what you want.

 Often, we'll hear actors talk about doing theatre "in order to" get more experience when they really want to have a film career. Why focus on theatre, when you want to do movies? What do you really want? When you think about it, what puts a big smile on your face? When we work with actors, we can always tell when a person is being sensible or overly reasonable as they do this exercise—there is something missing in their eyes. The minute they hit on the thing that they really want to create, there is a sparkle in their eyes and a big grin on their faces. So, what puts a smile on your face when you think about having it in your career?

 Let yourself have fun with this exercise. Go:

_____

_____

_____

_____

_____

_____

_____

_____

_____

_____

_____

_____
_____
_____
_____
_____
_____
_____
_____
_____
_____
_____
_____
_____
_____
_____
_____
_____
_____
_____
_____
_____
_____
_____
_____
_____
_____

Great. Now, the next step is to go back and pick one thing. If you wrote: "I want to win an academy award, get an agent, book a sitcom, book a movie, book a commercial"—GREAT! The best way to start creating your plan is to pick one area and then focus on it. Just as with learning how to juggle, you start with one ball at a time. By picking one area to focus your time, money, and energy on, you won't be distracted or pulled in different directions.

So, maybe as you read this, you are saying to yourself: "Yeah, but I want it all." You can have it all, but when building a business, it is easier to build one thing at a time. What often happens when people set "having it all" as a goal is that nothing gets done or the actions that are taken are not specific enough to create results.

Take at look at what you've written above and distill it down to a statement like the examples below:

Examples: I want to book a national commercial.

I want to have a lead in a movie.

I want a speaking role in a TV drama.

_____

_____

_____

_____

_____

_____

_____

_____

_____

_____

_____

_____

_____

_____

_____

_____

_____

_____

_____

_____

_____

_____

_____

_____

_____

Remember to always be clear with your language. Have you ever heard the saying "Be careful what you ask for you just might get it"? Since it is highly probable that you'll get what you are asking for, be clear and specific about what you ask for.

Years ago, an actor we know wanted a Broadway audition. She did everything she could to be seen for a specific production. She walked in to the office of the casting director for the production and even asked for the audition. Well, she got the audition—what she asked for. After the audition, she realized she wanted the audition and to book the role. Being specific is an important part of creating your plan and setting goals. You can get what you ask for when you ask for it specifically and are willing to **take the necessary actions** to support your intention. Remember, creating acting work is a combination of wishing and taking actions to support your dreams.

Another actress we know moved from New York to LA, and set her goal as getting two speaking roles on TV. Well, she got the two speaking roles . . . in commercials. What she really wanted was two speaking roles on episodic TV or a sitcom. Again, the point here is to **ask for what you want, clearly and specifically.**

If your goal is:

To be on a sitcom

A way to make it more specific is:

I would like to book a paying speaking role on a sitcom.

Let's say you have this goal:

I want an agent.

A way to make it more specific is:

I want a legit/theatrical agent who is excited about me and helping me promote my career.

Let's say you have this goal:

I want to work in movies.

A way to make it more specific is:

I will book a paying speaking role in an independent film.

In this next section clean up your goal, and be specific and clear:

_____

_____

_____

_____

_____

_____

_____

_____

_____

_____

_____

_____

_____

_____

_____

_____

_____

_____

_____

_____

_____

_____

_____

_____

_____

_____

_____

_____

_____

_____

_____

_____

_____

_____

_____

Now we need to add a time frame to your goal. For instance: This year I will get a speaking role on a sitcom. Or, I will book a lead in a national commercial in the next 6 months. The reason we add a time frame is to keep the goal in the "now." Keeping your goal in the "now" also helps you stay focused, because each day you have an idea of what action/s you can take that will move you closer to your desired outcome. Often people talk about their careers as something that will happen in the future. Today is not a dress rehearsal for your career. Having a specific goal allows you to focus on what you want to create—now. Think of it as having a personal roadmap for the journey you'll travel in your career.

Use this next section to add a timeline to your goal:

_____
_____
_____
_____
_____
_____
_____
_____
_____
_____
_____
_____
_____
_____
_____
_____
_____
_____
_____
_____
_____
_____
_____
_____
_____
_____
_____
_____
_____
_____

_____

_____

_____

_____

_____

_____

_____

_____

_____

_____

When working on your goal, please be aware that winning an Academy Award or getting an agent are two things that are a "part of" your goal. For example, let's say your goal is to work in films. An agent is there to help you achieve your goal; an agent is not the goal. Once you get an agent, what are you going to do to move your career forward? Are you just going to wait for the agent to phone with auditions? That would be nice, but chances are you'll be waiting for some time before the phone rings. Remember, you are one of many clients that an agent represents. An Academy Award is a reward for achieving the goal of working consistently in films; it too is not the goal. If you want an Academy Award, go for it, but you're going to have to focus on working in films in order to reach that goal. **So, focus on getting work in films and the agent and the Academy Award may come as a result of working in films and doing outstanding work in the films you get.**

An interesting goal setting measurement tool is a technique called **SMART** goals. SMART is an acronym for goals that are: specific, measurable, attainable, relevant, and time-based. Although your acting career goals originate from a place of joy, passion, and dreams, bringing your goals to fruition takes action and consistent work.

You can measure your PLAN in this way: A **specific** goal is simple and easy to describe. "I want to act" is not specific. "I want to act in a sitcom" is specific. The clearer you are, the easier it is to focus.

A **measurable** goal is one that has a specific outcome. How will you know when you've achieved your goal? For example, the goal of booking a commercial in a year is measurable. On December 31st you have either reached the goal or not.

An **attainable** goal is one that allows you to stretch, but is not impossible. Let's say you want the lead in a studio summer blockbuster film. Great goal. But, if currently you don't even have a headshot and resumé or have ever met with an agent, this goal is *currently* not achievable or attainable. If working in studio films is your goal, then perhaps the first step would be to find out what movies are in development, when they are going to be shot, and who is in charge of casting. Then, either ask your agent to get you an audition or you can contact the casting director directly (with the cover letter you learned how to write in Chapter 3). Think of your bigger goal and then break it down into "bite-size" doable segments.

A **relevant** goal is one that has meaning for you. It is not just a good idea or some well-meaning piece of advice you've gotten or suggestion that someone gives you. It reflects who you are and what you value as a human being. Again, pick something that gives YOU joy and allow yourself to dream. When thinking about working as an actor, no actor dreams about marketing or doing mailings or making phone calls asking for work—they dream about being the star in a movie or the lead in a play on-stage—so base your goal in something that inspires you, and then the marketing becomes easier to do. Why? Because the end outcome pulls you forward like a magnet.

A **time-based** goal is one that has an end date. Even if you don't know if you can accomplish your goal in the time you've set for yourself, set a date anyway. The mind responds to specifics. Setting a date and creating a plan or path for the goal will notify your mind you mean business!

One of the reasons that goal setting has such a bad reputation is that we often confuse a goal with a chore or something that has to be done (like laundry or dishes). If you don't experience a resounding "yes" as you create goals for yourself, then you are creating another variation of a "to-do list." Ask yourself: "Will I be relieved when it is done?" If the answer is yes to this question, you have a chore, not a goal. If you've made a list of chores for yourself, they do not belong in your plan.

An interesting outcome of pursuing your goal may be the potential of more acting work. **Work tends to breed work.** So, even though you are working toward a gig on a sitcom, you'll find that you may get offered other opportunities to work. If you are a beginning actor it makes sense to experience these opportunities. Why? The more you work, the more your confidence will grow and the more comfortable you'll be in the professional community. You will also become known and get to know more people in the acting world.

Before stepping into these new opportunities, always be clear about what you are getting into. If the opportunity takes you too far from your preferred goal path, then maybe it isn't the right opportunity for you at this moment in time. If it requires a short time commitment on your part, if there is a great part available, if the director is someone you want to work with, if the script excites you—then step into the opportunity that is being presented to you as you pursue your primary objective.

But remember, be clear about why you are taking the work and what is expected of you regarding time. There are 24 hours in a day, and if you spend time doing something that isn't moving you toward your primary goal, how will it benefit you? This is the question you need to ask yourself when new opportunities for work present themselves. **How will you benefit? If you say "yes" to this opportunity, what's in it for you?**

Here is a checklist that you can use when deciding whether an opportunity is right for you:

1. Will you grow as an actor and artist?
2. Do I need this job for the experience? Will having more experience help my confidence as an actor?
3. Who will you be working with and will you be establishing relationships or connections that can lead to work in the future?
4. Is there a salary and will you earn money as an actor?
5. Will you get exposure that can lead to future jobs? (i.e., where will the final product/project be shown?)
6. Do you love the script and the part you've been offered?
7. What kind of time commitment does this project entail? For example, how much time for rehearsal is expected and will that affect your day job and income?
8. Does the director and production team look organized? Is there a script? Is there a storyboard for you to look at? Is it a professional group with a track record of productions that is offering you this opportunity or is it a first-time director that has big ideas and no training? Everyone needs to start somewhere, but if you have to wait on someone's "vision" on set or in rehearsal, it is highly likely you'll be waiting and wasting your valuable time as you wait.
9. Will the credit look good on your resumé? Do you need more credits for your resumé?
10. Do you have anything going on right now? If the answer to this question is "no," then it could be a good idea to take on the opportunity. It is always good to be working on something as an actor. You'll feel better about yourself and your career.

If you are clear there are benefits to you, then it is worth taking on work that may take you away from your primary goal because **the journey you take toward reaching your goal is rarely a straight path.** As with anything in life or business, sometimes you may need to take two steps to the side or backward in order to bring yourself forward. The important thing to remember is that not every opportunity offered to you is worth your time.

Here's an example of taking a step back in order to take a step forward: let's say your goal is to work in television; if your training is primarily in theatre, then taking an on-camera TV course is a step to the side that will move you forward. Or what about the scenario where you aren't getting ANY callbacks. You are going to auditions and no one is inviting you back to read again for round two. In this case, an audition class is a good idea that is a step to the side so that you can move forward toward your goal. Another example of how this works would be: you are offered a role in an off-off Broadway show where the lead is a soap actress who has a thriving career. She is being positioned in the industry to be the "next big thing." You have no interest in working in theatre, but by taking on this project you are guaranteed to be seen by people who are there to see the soap opera actress. Her connections become a stepping stone toward your career goals.

Now that we have the goal, you are probably wondering "what's next?" You may be thinking: "It is all fine and good to write out my dreams, but that won't actually get me the gig." **So the next step is to create the action steps that will move you forward toward your goal.** The rest of this chapter will introduce you to various goal setting techniques that will help give you structure for your action steps.

Creating Your Plan: Designing Your Action Steps

There is no specific order to the following techniques. Look them over, see which one seems interesting and fun to you, and then give it a try. You can always revisit this chapter at a later date and try another technique. When it comes to goal setting, one size does not fit all. But, at the foundation of all goal setting is ACTION. When you complete this chapter, you should have a set of clear, specific action steps that you can take to move your career forward.

Brainstorming is a technique where it is the quantity of the ideas, not the quality of the ideas that is important. During the brainstorming process you DO NOT EDIT OR CENSOR your ideas. You write everything down and allow yourself to look at it as a possibility.

Here is an example of how this could work when using brainstorming as a way of creating your action plan:

My goal is to get cast in a well-paying speaking role in a sitcom within the next year. (If you set the goal in March, give yourself 365 days from the date you set the goal as your target date for reaching the goal.)

Then sit down for at least 20 minutes and start writing. Here's what a potential brainstorming list might look like:

- Make a list of the casting directors who cast sitcoms
- Write a personal letter to each one introducing yourself and describing yourself.
- Join an improv group.
- Have a funny postcard made up and send it to casting directors or agents that specialize in comedic talent.
- Begin to write letters to the directors of sitcoms.
- Do some stand-up.
- Go to the casting director workshops in your area; meet the casting directors who cast sitcoms.
- Go to a taping in LA or New York of a sitcom.
- Write your own pilot.

Based on the list above, there are a lot of ideas for you with regard to actions you can take to reach your goal. So, where do you start first? We will look at this in Chapter 7, "Putting the Plan into Action."

Now it is your turn. Write your goal down and do some brainstorming:

_____

_____

_____

_____

_____

_____

_____

_____

_____

_____

_____

_____

_____

_____

_____

_____

_____

_____

_____
_____
_____
_____
_____
_____
_____
_____
_____
_____
_____
_____
_____
_____
_____
_____
_____
_____
_____
_____
_____
_____
_____
_____
_____
_____
_____
_____
_____
_____

Something else to consider is that brainstorming can also be done in a group format. First, select someone whose goal will be focused on, then have that person simply write down what each person suggests; go around the group at least three to four times throwing out ideas. Each group member will take at least 3 to 4 turns throwing out ideas for your goal. Each person in the group should get about 15 to 20 minutes.

Another interesting way of using the brainstorming technique is to write out 50 things you can immediately do to reach your goal. Somewhere around the 25th or 30th item your brain starts to open up and ideas you hadn't considered before start to surface. The key to this approach is that you have fun. No idea is too far-fetched or out there, at least not in this phase.

Try a stream of consciousness exercise. What do you want to do, have, be, accomplish in your career in 1 week, 1 month, 6 months, 1 year, 5 years, 10 years, or 20 years? Write out about 10 items for each increment of time. The entire exercise should last a total of 20 or 30 minutes. The value of this exercise is letting the intuitive part of your brain inform you as to what you want to create in your career.

Notice if there are any themes or activities that keep occurring as you do this exercise. Pay attention to what keeps showing up, because these are the areas you want to concentrate on. As with other exercises in this book, do not make a "to-do list." This stream of consciousness exercise is another approach to brainstorming. It can help you access what is important to you. The more in touch you are with what turns you on as an artist, the easier it will be to take the necessary actions to make your career a reality.

Here is an example of how this exercise can work:

In 1 week:	I'd like to find a good acting class.
	I'd like to find an agent.
	I'd like to go on an audition.
In 1 month:	I'd like to be called by an agent.
	I'd like to be taking a class with a great teacher.
	I'd like to be going to one audition a week.
In 6 months:	I'd like to book an acting job.
	I'd like to have had at least two agent meetings.
	I'd like to be known by two casting directors.
In 1 year:	I'd like to be working on paying projects three times per year.
	I'd like to be working with an agent who knows me and respects my work.
	I'd like to be known by six casting directors who call me in when I'm right for a project.
In 5 years:	I would like to be called in regularly because my work and my type are known by casting directors.
	I'd like to be making 65% of my income as an actor.
	I am a member of all the acting unions.

Please continue with this exercise and do the 10- and 20-year increments as well. Notice that the recurring themes in the above example are: casting directors, agents, working regularly as a professional, and growing as an artist.

So, how does this translate into actions? One approach to designing an action step would be to look through the trades each week and see what classes are being offered. This will take care of growing yourself as an artist. Also, when looking through the trades (i.e., *Backstage* and/or any of the online audition websites) look for auditions. Auditioning and then booking the work will lead to connecting with an agent because agents prefer working proactive actors.

This stream of consciousness exercise helps you see the bigger picture of your career. As you do this exercise you'll begin to notice that you favor certain topics, and that is where you want to focus your attention, energy, and actions.

Also, when doing this, don't forget to mention the type of work (i.e., commercials, theatre, film) and location (do you want to stay in your market or move to LA or NY?). Be open to what surfaces for you in this exercise and again DO NOT CENSOR YOURSELF.

Your turn:

_____

_____

_____

_____

_____

_____

_____

_____

_____

_____

_____

_____

_____

_____

_____

_____

_____

_____

_____

_____

_____

_____

_____
_____
_____
_____
_____
_____
_____
_____
_____
_____
_____
_____
_____

Another technique you can use is to make a **career map.** For those of you who are visual, this exercise is for you. If "arts and crafts" was your favorite class in school, this exercise is one you'll enjoy using to brainstorm. Our minds love to respond to symbols and images. Advertising is built on this premise. Think about doing this technique with a partner or a small group—it is a fun and entertaining approach to designing goals and makes marketing yourself as an actor seem more accessible.

1. Before you start this exercise, you'll need to collect and save a variety of industry magazines and general interest magazines.
2. Take a large piece of paper (or poster board if you are feeling especially artistic).
3. Start looking through the magazines and cut out whatever images or words grab your attention.
4. Paste these images to your paper or board. Don't be shy; you can use glitter and other color enhancements as you design your future. If dollar signs keep grabbing your attention, cut them out.
5. Put in milestones. These milestones are rewards you get each time you have a professional success (like booking an acting job). Advent calendars are designed in this way. Each day you get to open a door on the calendar and underneath you'll generally find a piece of chocolate or a small prize. So, once you start reaching milestones, give yourself rewards like a massage, a new pair of shoes, or the newest video game.
6. When you've finished creating your career map, place it somewhere that you can see it on a regular basis and continue working on your career (networking, marketing, taking classes, submitting headshots

and resumés). Continue taking action and keep the career map at the periphery of your awareness.

Let your imagination guide you as you create a visual road map for your desired outcomes. Again, do not censor yourself as you do this work.

In case you are wondering whether this technique works, the book you are currently reading is a product of this exercise. The creation of this book was not a linear path, but the seeds of the book it has now become started years ago when we made a career map. Why do we mention this to you at this juncture? Because, **the journey you take toward reaching your goal is rarely a straight path.**

Here is another technique you can use: **backward goal setting**. If one of your acting teachers, a good friend, or one of the authors bumped into you next year at this time, after you've traded small talk, what would you say that you had achieved in your career in the past year? Think about it, **12 months from today, what work will you have done as an actor?**

Once you answer that question, start to work backward: what will you have to do at 9 months, 6 months, at 3 months, at 1 month, and in the next week to have created this outcome?

Here is how this works, let's say your goal is to:

Be cast in a paying speaking role on a soap opera.

At 9 months what will you have to do to achieve this goal?

Booked an extra job on soap and networked (in a professional way— remember, no stalking) while you were on set.

At 6 months what will you have to do to achieve this goal?

Have made contact at least once with everyone on the list you made at 1 month. And, followed up with at least 3 to 5 people you've already contacted or have met.

At 3 months what will you have to do to achieve this goal?

Have completed an introductory mailing to all soap opera casting directors in your area. And, found a way to meet at least three casting directors (i.e., classes, workshops, etc.).

At 1 month, what will you have to do to achieve this goal?

Become familiar with what soap operas are cast in your area. Get to know the names of the casting directors of each soap opera.

At 1 week:

Watched at least 3 to 4 hours of soap operas to find out what the storylines entail, to see what kinds of actors are used in soap operas, and to
learn what kinds of characters inhabit the stories.

Your turn:

9 months:

_____

_____

_____

_____

_____

_____

_____

_____

_____

_____

_____

_____

_____

_____

_____

_____

_____

_____

_____

_____

_____

_____

_____

_____

_____

_____

_____

_____

_____

_____

_____

6 months:

_____

_____

_____

_____

_____

_____

_____

_____

_____

_____

_____

_____

_____

_____

_____

_____

_____

_____

_____

_____

_____

_____

_____

_____

_____

_____

_____

3 months:

_____

_____

_____

_____

_____

_____

_____

_____
_____
_____
_____
_____
_____
_____
_____
_____
_____
_____
_____
_____
_____
_____
_____
_____
_____
_____
_____
_____

1 month:

_____
_____
_____
_____
_____
_____
_____
_____
_____
_____
_____
_____

_____

_____

_____

_____

_____

_____

_____

_____

_____

_____

_____

_____

_____

There are many creativity techniques that can help you get clear about your goals and support you in creating your plan. Each person has a preferred way of brainstorming. What works for one person does not necessarily work for someone else. The bottom line here is to find a way that works for you and to start working on it. You can't have a plan without action steps.

Another benefit of approaching your goal setting in this way is that you have the tools to consistently generate your own ideas. It can be difficult to think of ways to keep yourself moving and growing when it comes to the business of acting—using these creative approaches will help build up a reserve of actions to take. You no longer have to wait for someone to help you figure out what's next for you in your career because you now have the ability to create your own answers.

If you are wondering how you can a create plan for your acting career if you don't live in one of the major markets (LA, New York, Chicago, Orlando, or Dallas), here is a list of action steps an actress in Kansas City, Missouri, has taken. Her goal was to work in commercials within a calendar year. The action steps she took to support this goal were:

1. Sent her picture and resumé to all the casting departments of the advertising agencies in Kansas City.
2. Dropped off her picture and resumé to all the talent agencies in Kansas City.
3. Researched casting directors and discovered that three casting directors worked out of a Kansas City home and mailed her headshot and resumé to all three.

4. She shot a commercial demo reel where she performed a commercial and mailed this demo to the agents and casting directors so they could see her working in a commercial.

5. Researched and mailed her materials to the video production houses that produced commercials locally.

6. Contacted the corporate headquarters of companies that are based in or around Kansas City and sent her materials to their in-house advertising agencies.

7. Made a voice-over demo tape and dropped it off to recording studios in Kansas City.

If you are looking for production house information in the city you live in, check out *www.productionhub.com*.

Again, the principles you are learning in this book can be applied to any market. For example, if you want to work in films, most every city now has a film commission. Want to work in theatre? Check out your local community theatre for possible leads. Your local Yellow Pages are a great source of information. You need to become a detective in order to find the acting work that is available in your community. You can find acting work, even if you don't live in New York or LA, but you'll need to work to find it.

So, what is YOUR goal?

_____

_____

_____

_____

_____

_____

_____

_____

_____

_____

_____

_____

_____

_____

_____

_____

_____

_____

_____
_____
_____
_____
_____
_____
_____
_____
_____
_____
_____
_____
_____
_____
_____
_____
_____
_____

What actions will you take to make it happen?

1. _____

2. _____

3. _____

4. _____

5. _____

6. _____

7. _____

8. _____

9. _____

10. _____

The important thing to remember here is: ACTION. Take action. Find what works for you and what you enjoy doing and then do it, over and over and over, until you start to move forward in your career.

Now, you are ready to put your plan into action and move on to the next chapter.

7 Putting the Plan into Action

So, now that you have your plan (remember, we define plan as a goal and the action steps needed to make it happen), **NOW WHAT?** Having a plan is important, but without actually doing something about The Plan, your plan is simply a piece of paper with words on it, it is not a flourishing acting career. Yes, you need a plan, but you also have to **put your plan in motion.**

How do you put a plan into action?

One method is to **keep business hours.** Every day you sit down in your work area and you take steps to get acting work. For example, you read the trades, look for auditions, put a picture and resumé in the mail, make a business phone call, go to an audition, or upload your headshot and resumé to a website. Given that most actors need to work a side job in order to put food on the table and a roof over their heads, your schedule might change from week to week. Consider writing your business hours on your calendar as if you had a scheduled appointment at that time. Make an appointment with yourself for your business and for success. What is important here is that you **consistently work on and in your business and you clear a space in your schedule for it to happen.**

Another method for jump-starting your plan is to **take one action a day.** Remember, these actions are not about improving your acting technique, although this too is crucial for getting work as an actor, the daily action suggested here is one specific thing you do each day from a business standpoint in order to create work opportunities. An example of how this works is found in a fable called "The Tortoise and the Hare." In this fable the Hare and Tortoise have a race. The Hare takes off, laughing at how slow the Tortoise is. He gets so far ahead of the Tortoise, he figures he can take a little nap. Guess what, the Tortoise passes him and wins the race. This fable has been around for at least 1,000 years, so this advice has been working for a very long time. Don't discount single daily actions and the momentum they can give you. Slow and steady is a strategy you can use to win the race.

Another approach you can use as you put your plan into action is to **set a goal of five actions a week.** You can do all five in one afternoon if your schedule permits, or you can do it over a couple of days, or you can do one business related action each day. Let's do the math: if you take five actions every week with two weeks off a year (for vacation), you'll have taken **250 actions over a one-year period.** If you've done your marketing correctly YOU WILL get auditions and work. If you've taken the steps advocated in previous chapters of this book, you'll find you are marketing yourself correctly. If your headshot looks like you on a good day; if you aren't submitting yourself for parts you are not right for; if you understand what makes you unique as an actor and artist and are submitting yourself for roles that match your age, look, type, and interests—then you are marketing yourself correctly. If you take 250 actions in one year that are business related and focused on getting work, something will happen for you.

A key factor in helping you put your plan into action is **setting up an office or work space.** This is an area in your home that is actor friendly— your headshots are easily accessible, your resumés are ready to attach to your headshots, your envelopes are nearby, you've got enough postage to mail your headshots without going to the post office every time you want to put a picture and resumé in the mail, you've got a relatively clutter-free desk to work at, you've got fax capability, stationery, a reliable computer with current software on it, and plenty of room to work. When you sit down to work on your career, you have a space that makes the work easy to do.

Next, you'll need to develop what we call a **HIT LIST.** Your Hit List consists of 30 to 50 names. The names on the list are people working in the industry or those that can potentially help you book acting work. The Hit List is a focused list of people who you want to get to know and who should know about you and your work and they have the potential of moving you closer to your goal.

You'll need to have some reference materials to start creating your HIT LIST. Using a *Ross Report* is a good place to start, but there are also plenty of other books out there. K. Callan's books are another good source of information for creating a list of names. You'll find a list of books and resources you can use for marketing purposes at the back of this book. Once you have your resource materials, start by looking at the casting directors that are listed. For instance, if your goal is to be on a sitcom, write down all of the casting directors that cast sitcoms.

You will see that the same casting directors tend to cast similar projects. For example, Zane/Pillsbury Casting in Los Angeles has cast a number of sitcoms over a 20-year period. Shows they've cast are: *According to Jim, The*

George Lopez Show, Mad About You, and *Sports Night.* Another point to take into consideration as you create your Hit List is that even though a show gets canceled and the casting director does not have work for you today, this same person will work again, so grow your professional relationships and stay in contact with people who have the potential and ability to give you work. As you build your Hit List consider adding writers, agents, producers, and directors.

When building your Hit List, don't forget that there are "six degrees of separation." You never know who you know that (1) knows someone who can either give you work or (2) point you in the direction of work or (3) a relationship that can lead to work. Your mother's friend may have a friend who has a cousin who works in the film industry. Whether this person actually becomes a business contact or not, what is important here is that it is easier to build business relationships when there is some connection rather than starting cold.

Remember, your Hit List is a work in progress. Names can and will change. You will always be learning new names and people as they come and go from this industry on a regular basis, so your list needs to change with the changing cast of characters.

So, who is going to go on your hit list?

HIT LIST:

_____

_____

_____

_____

_____

_____

_____

_____

_____

_____

_____

_____

_____

_____

_____

_____

_____

_____

_____

_____
_____
_____
_____
_____
_____
_____
_____
_____
_____
_____
_____
_____
_____
_____
_____
_____
_____
_____
_____
_____

Another reason that having a Hit List is a valuable approach to putting your plan into action is that it is a cost-effective approach to marketing. Every time you do a mailing, you don't have to mail to everyone in the *Ross Reports*. There are easily 300 names listed in the *Ross Reports* for each coast that you can mail to. It is simply too expensive to mail to every person in the directory on a regular basis.

It is more effective to focus on building relationships with people that are working in the area you want to be working. For example, if there is a casting director that specializes in casting male character actors who range in age from 35 to 50, and you are a blond, blue-eyed, cheerleader-looking, type from the Midwest, is it smart to spend your marketing money mailing to this casting director? Yes, there could be a role for you in one of their projects, but wouldn't you rather reach out to someone that you know specializes in your type and is casting the kinds of projects you want to be doing? **Do the initial mass mailings that introduce you to the industry in your community** (i.e., Los Angeles, New York, Chicago, Florida, wherever you live). The function of a mass mailing is to introduce you to potential buyers of your skills. **Then, focus on creating a Hit List. It will save you money over the long term.**

Remember, all business is about relationships. Working on getting to know the people on your Hit List helps you build relationships.

Do not lose sight of the fact that the names on your list are people first and industry contacts second. Like you, they are either looking for work, trying to do good work at their current job, or are interested in spending more time with their family or spouses and having a good life. Like you, they are people who are doing a job. What makes them different than you is that they have access to opportunities you want. Create a Hit List, build professional relationships, and you'll find yourself moving toward accomplishing your career goals.

Once you start taking actions on a consistent basis, you'll need a way to track the data you generate and the actions you take.

Tracking Your Progress

Here are some methods you can use to organize the action steps you are taking, the networking you are doing, and the contacts you are making:

1. You can find **audition logs/contact logs** at the drama bookstores in your community. You can also make your own, using a simple notebook.
2. Develop a **database** on your computer or look for computer programs that are designed for actors and tracking their progress. ActorTrak is one example of a career management program you can use. Find out more about it at: *www.holdonlog.com.*
3. Get a file box and index cards and at the top of each card, write a contact's name, mailing address, and phone number. Each time you connect with them in any way (an audition, a mailing, a meeting), write the date and what happened.

Here is an example of what an index card could like:

John Lee Casting Director Address and phone
2/07—met @ Cold reading workshop—did scene from *Deer Hunter*
2/07—wrote thank-you note.
4/07—sent another letter letting him know that I'm now performing improv once a month and invited him to see me.
7/07—Sent him a postcard about the play I'm doing and invited him to see me.
9/07—called me in for audition for play he is casting.
9/07—wrote thank-you for audition.

Think of the above categories as a way of organizing your spreadsheet if you decide to design your own spreadsheet/database.

It doesn't matter what system you pick (database, notebooks, or index cards). What does matter is that you organize your contacts and the interactions you have with the potential buyers of your services. **Once you meet someone and make a connection with them, stay in contact with them.**

An actress we know auditioned for a casting director in New York in the 80s, who at that time predominately cast theatre projects. This same casting director now casts *Heroes* on NBC. This casting director also cast the now-canceled shows: *Crossing Jordan* and *American Dreams* (by the way, both of which were also on NBC). When this actress moved to LA, she found out that this same casting director was now casting episodic TV for a major network. She wrote the casting director a note reminding her of their past meetings in New York and now the actress is being called in on a regular basis for prime-time television. Who would think that an index card started 20 years ago could lead to auditions today? Tracking your contacts works.

People can stay in this business a long time and once again we remind you that all business is about relationships. So, the casting director you meet today who likes your work, but doesn't necessarily cast you, can lead to possible work in the future—but you have to stay in contact with him or her. **Whatever tracking system you choose to use, make sure it has longevity.**

Here's an example of how longevity and tracking benefited our students: a few years ago two actresses delivered cookies to various casting offices in New York to promote a play they were doing. They managed to get into all kinds of offices, including ABC, *and* they had a blast passing out the cookies. Even though the method of marketing was creative and unusual, both actresses were professional and called each office and let the person answering the phone know they were delivering cookies. Once the person heard the word *cookies*, their names were delivered to the front desk and they were allowed access to the offices. Please note that in today's world climate, you may have to take a few extra steps to make in-person contact with someone who can potentially cast you, but if handled professionally, you can do it.

Everyone loved the cookies and they made some great contacts that day. One of their last stops was to a notoriously mean casting director. They dropped off the cookies to her assistants and were in the hallway regrouping when the casting director stormed out, handed them their cookies, and proclaimed "This office does not accept cookies!"

The first lesson in this story is: If they had been by themselves, they would have forgotten about all the positive work and connections they had achieved earlier in the day and instead would have concentrated on the one bad interaction they had experienced and what negative repercussions could happen from it. Instead, because they were together, they had a great laugh about the "Cookie Monster" and ended their day on a high note with laughter.

The second lesson that came from this experience happened a few months ago. One of the actresses was called in by a prestigious casting director for a high-profile movie. During her audition, he mentioned that he had been an assistant in the "Cookie Monster's" office the day she and her friend had delivered the cookies. He was so embarrassed by his boss's behavior, that he made a point of remembering the actresses' names. He had been tracking both of their careers for close to 10 years. No, they weren't a priority in terms of his work, but they were definitely on his radar. As we keep mentioning, all business is about relationships and he remembered one of the actresses and when he had a part she was right for, he called her in. Remember, the secretary that answers the phone today could become an important casting director in the next few years. It happens all the time.

It's important to remember that staying on the radar of casting directors who specialize in casting features can lead to work. Unfortunately, it may take 5 years before you get called in, but it will eventually deliver opportunities. Think about it, a casting director that specializes in films may work on one or two projects a year and there simply may not be a role for you in the films they're casting. So, by staying in contact with a casting director that works on the types of projects you want to be in (for example, low-budget, edgy independent films), you increase your chances of being called in for an audition.

Stay in contact with casting people when you have something to report, for example, a new show, a booking, an important callback, an amazing new class with a special teacher, or new headshots. Do not touch base just to say "hi." Remember, be professional. Just as their career is growing, demonstrate that your career is growing and evolving as well. **A general rule of thumb is to stay in contact with your Hit List every 6 to 8 weeks when you have something to report.** Do not overdo it; overexposure is a possibility. Think about when you keep being hounded to do something, how do you react? Would you like an industry professional to think that about you? Do not overdo it.

Another important skill to develop as an actor is your investigative abilities. **Be a detective; learn how to track people's careers.** What is the name of the person who has the potential to give you work? For example, do you take the time to learn the names of people who cast the films you like? As soon as the house lights come up in the movie theatre, are you up and out of the theatre? If you are, you are missing the names of the people who cast the film and contributed to the experience you just enjoyed. Start looking around you and you'll begin to see that the same names keep showing up in movies, in sitcoms, and episodic TV. We gave you an example of this earlier in the chapter. Another way to approach detective work is to notice trends in the industry. For example, directors who do music videos have started becoming feature film directors. For example, McG directed music videos and is now directing the Charlie's Angels movies. Spike Jonze and David Fincher also have made this crossover. Learn the names of people who do work you admire and put them on your Hit List. The point here is no one is going to tell you who to contact. Even if you have an agent, it is still your responsibility to know your industry.

One way to make sure that you are consistent in your marketing and tracking is to find a way to make it fun for you. The marketing is a means to an end, but if the marketing isn't fun for you, you won't do it.

Jay Perry developed a game you can use for tracking your contacts and goals called The Fan Club Game. If you'd like to find out more about the game, you can go to: *www.playthegameof.com/bookstore.html* and click on The Fan Club Game icon. Jay has been working with actors since the early 80's. As part of the game, you create a GAMEBOARD.

Your GAMEBOARD can look something like this:

Stranger	*Awareness*	*Pen Pal*	*Audition*	*Call Back*	*Hire*	*Fan Club*
Casting Director						
Casting Director						
Agent						
Agent						

The idea of this game is to move as many contacts as possible across the board and into your Fan Club. In the above example:

Stranger: Someone who you do not know and who does not know you.

Awareness: Someone that you've made the effort to meet or at least have written a letter introducing yourself to this person.

Pen Pal: Someone that you've started to develop a business relationship with. You've gotten a phone call from them; you've established some kind of face-to-face connection with them. They recognize you when you meet with them.

Audition: This person has called you in. This is a good thing. That means your marketing is working and you are actually out there getting interviews.

Callback: This is an even better thing for you; you are making it to round two and are closer to actually booking the work. Although booking the job is better than a callback, a callback is still useful to you, because you can leverage it in your marketing materials. Basically, you are saying: "Look who is interested in me and my work." When you reach the callback stage, things are simply out of your control as to who finally gets the part. With callbacks, you know that you are definitely being considered.

Hire: Congratulations, you've booked the job.

Fan Club: When someone is a fan of yours, you are on the short list of candidates they consider when working on a project. They know you, they like your work, they like you as a person, and they know you'll deliver. Someone who is a fan of yours is different than someone who hires you. A fan is someone who believes in your talent. Someone who is your fan will keep bringing you in, whether you are hired or not. Years ago, a commercial casting director called in an actress we know over a 2-year period. She didn't book any of the commercials she auditioned for, but they kept calling her in because they believed in her and knew it was only a question of time before she broke out professionally.

You can use the previous categories for your Gameboard, or you can choose any categories that you want. The purpose of the Gameboard is to track the progression of your industry contacts. Go ahead, be creative and create a tracking system that is fun and that you'll keep using.

So, you get excited, you do a mailing, you set up a Gameboard, and then you notice that you are doing less and less for your career. You start to notice that you are spending more and more time in front of the TV playing video games and eating potato chips and that it is getting harder and harder to stay focused. Now what?

Accountability

Accountability gives structure to the goals you set. Early in the book, we mention that there is no need to go it alone in this business and your marketing and tracking are no exceptions. There is strength in numbers. Find a marketing buddy, create an accountability group, hire a business coach—set up structures outside yourself that will keep you focused. An example of this: A student wanted to write a one-person theatre piece and was making no progress toward her goal. The goal inspired and excited her, but not enough to get her moving toward her goal. She then enrolled in a writing workshop that had specific deadlines and homework assignments and that helped her succeed in completing her one-act play. She needed external structure in order to help her focus her energy, and succeed.

Now, ask yourself who is going to hold you accountable for getting your work done. If the answer is no one, then consider forming an **accountability group.**

This is a group of peers that meets once a week or every couple of weeks and consists of people you know from acting school, acting classes, or even your restaurant job. What is important here is that everyone in the group has a plan and is committed to creating success in their artistic careers. When you meet, make sure you have an agenda. The group has a social element, but the emphasis needs to be on helping you and the other members of the group stay focused on getting work. Don't let local boundaries define who is in your accountability group. You don't have to meet face-to-face; you can have people from all over the world be part of your group because of today's technology.

Your agenda could look something like this:

1. What have I been doing?
2. What have I not been doing?
3. What do I intend to do before the next meeting?
4. What do I need support on?
5. Am I feeling challenged in any area?
6. What successes do I have do report to the group?
7. Am I not taking any action on the goals I say are important to me? Is something getting in the way?

Having a plan and the action steps that will bring it into reality are the foundation for building a career, but if you don't find a way to make it fun yourself, or at least tolerable, you won't stay focused. You will lose your interest and enthusiasm for the work involved in finding acting work. There is no such thing as an overnight success. Finding work is a process so use your creativity or any of the methods we've introduced you to, but definitely find a way that works for you and stay in action.

In case you do lose your enthusiasm, the next chapter looks at techniques you can use to keep going when the going gets tough.

8 Staying Afloat

No matter how much fun you are having in your career or with your marketing you will encounter speed bumps along your journey. It is okay to get discouraged, but don't let it stop you. Everyone encounters "dry spells" during their career. Everyone has difficult phases in their careers, even stars who have achieved success at a high level. John Travolta is one example of an actor who has experienced this in a career that has spanned more than three decades.

Every actor, no matter where they are in their career or at what level they are working, experiences periods of time when there is nothing happening. You can either give in to despondency and frustration or you can assess the situation and do something about it.

Here are the authors' personal stories regarding this particular challenge that every actor experiences as they pursue acting work:

From Valorie: I realized the other day when coaching a client that there has to be a healthy mix of business and craft. My client told me that she had "burned out" on the business. I remember that I had told her to audition for some plays or small films earlier that year and she had not done that. I had suggested auditioning for these things because I thought she should be acting and not just looking for acting work. All she was doing was the marketing side and not experiencing the joy of creating and acting.

When I first moved to LA, I thought I knew everything about marketing considering I had created a flourishing career in New York from my marketing efforts. Well, I soon burned out on marketing in LA and wondered why. Maybe the burnout had to do with the fact that I work hard to get everything I book or maybe it had to do with the fact I'm not a 19-year-old starting out in Los Angeles. But no—that wasn't it. In New York, I had always been doing something creatively, whether it was a play or a scene or a movie or a commercial—I was always ACTING. Because I was working creatively and connected to my passion for acting, doing a mailing was effortless and fun, because my creative juices were already running at a high level. When I moved to LA, the auditions were few and far between so the creativity level went down and it became harder and harder to do or care about a mailing or casting director workshops. Recently I started booking work and I am ready to a do a mailing again—a coincidence? I don't think so. As a side note, a postcard mailing I did recently to promote a film I've done led to an audition for a national commercial.

From Lea: As a performer, I can't think of anything worse than waiting for the phone to ring. Sometimes it seems as if even if I was the last actor on the planet that the phone wouldn't ring with an audition or booking. Sometimes I'll even check to make sure my phone is still working, because if it is broken, then that's got to be the reason I'm not getting any calls for auditions or work. And when I'm in one of those "dry spells" I tend to forget that they can and will end eventually—and that in the meantime, there are things I can be doing to keep myself fit as a performer. I teach and direct to stay connected to my creativity.

As a teacher, I'm always reading scripts. And, as a teacher, I'm helping young actors work through their acting problems. As I help them, I help myself as an actress. I watch my students struggle with some of the same acting issues I have had to deal with over the years. As a director, I'm challenging myself to tell stories from a visual standpoint for film.

As an actress, I am inspired by actors who continue to act late in their lives. One of my role models is Doris Roberts. She won an Emmy for her work on the sitcom *Everybody Loves Raymond*. She won the Emmy in her late 60s playing his mother. Of course, I don't want to wait that long for my accolades, but it is good to know that it is possible that if you keep showing up, success can come to you. Another role model I have is Nancy Marchand. Go ahead, look her up at *www.imdb.com*. She worked for over 50 years as an actress. How wonderful is that—to do what you love for half a century? Her last role is that of Tony Soprano's mother on The Sopranos. In the story, Tony's mother passes away. In real life, Nancy Marchand passed away at that time. Think about it, someone writing a part for you and catering it to your needs. Now that in my opinion is something to look forward to as an actor. Your work is so respected, that people change shoot schedules to be able to work with you.

So, how do you handle the difficult cycles?

If you are experiencing a dry spell, **try doing an inventory of your business, marketing materials, and acting skills.** In business, an inventory is an itemized list of current assets. You look at what you have "in stock" and what you are missing and need to add to keep your business afloat and your customers (your team) happy. An inventory is an assessment of what is working for you and what is not working for you. Because you are the product being sold in your acting business, do not judge yourself as you engage in this inventory process. Remember, what you are doing here is measuring the tools of your business—not who you are as a human being. This is not about are you a good person or not, it is about you looking at your business and trying to figure out what adjustments, if any, need to be made.

Here are a few areas for you to consider as you begin your inventory:

1. Is your picture good? Does it really reflect you and your personality? Often, changing a headshot can break a dry spell. For example, recently two actors we know changed their headshots and started getting called in for auditions. In the first case, the actor changed his look from clean-cut, all-American guy to a scruffy, slacker look. In the other instance, the actor changed his look from glossy model to a good-looking guy you'd like to get to know. Do not change your photo if you send it out once or twice and get no response. You do not have enough data to make the assessment that it is time to get new headshots.

2. Does your resumé need to be updated? Many actors simply forget to update and upgrade their resumés. Some still have high school credits on their resumé when they can be replaced with stronger college and/or professional credits. Any new acting class you've taken needs to be added to your resumé. As mentioned in the resumé chapter, your acting resumé is a work in progress. Keep your resumé current and weed out the less attractive credits. Consider upgrading the quality of paper you use for your resumé. Don't use gimmicks when you upgrade your paper—a bright pink resumé will call attention to you in a way that probably won't help you in the long run. But what about selecting paper stock that has a "good feel" to it (for example, a cream-colored, 24-lb. paper)? If you don't know what this means, go to your local office supply store and really look at the paper stock. Consider creating a more visually appealing layout for your resumé that invites the viewer to actually take the time to read your resumé. Think about when you look through ads in a newspaper or on the web, what catches your eye? Certain ads make you want to look at them because of their visual composition. If laying out text on a page is a challenge to you or is of no interest to you, then think about hiring a graphic artist to help you. Consider using a different font style for your resumé. Be creative without being over the top.

3. Are you including a cover letter when you submit your picture and resumé? Often, actors just shove their picture and resumé in an

envelope expecting the reader to know exactly what they want. Don't underestimate the power of the personal connection your cover letter can create with the reader. Actors we work with have reported to us that because of the cover letter the actor included with their headshot, the actor was called in to audition.

For every anecdote or example we cite, know that you will hear the opinions of other industry people who say exactly the opposite. Please, take it all with a grain of salt. If 9 out of 10 people who you respect in the industry tell you a similar piece of information, then listen. If 9 out of 10 each tell you something different, then take it with a grain of salt. Ask yourself, what would you rather hear? How not to do your career or hearing an example that has and could give you the results you desire?

4. Is the cover letter you currently send out helping you or do you need to upgrade the content of your letter? If you are sending out a letter that simply says you are responding to an ad or heard that someone is casting a project and would like to be considered, that is not a good cover letter. A good cover letter creates a visual picture of you through the content, promotes you and your successes without arrogance, and makes a direct request of the reader. Don't forget to add your callbacks to your cover letter. You can't put a callback on a resumé, but you can still use that information on a cover letter. Just like your resumé, remember to update your cover letter.

5. Are you sending into anything and everything and not to things you are right for? Remember, knowing your type and focusing in on people who can use your skills will lead to results. Don't get frantic and start sending in your headshot and resumé hoping that there is a part for you. Be selective.

6. Are you submitting to projects that have already been cast and somehow the ad is still running? Do your homework and give yourself a break. You won't know this is happening or if it is happening—all you'll see is the end result. No one is calling you in for auditions. This is one of the variables in the industry that you have no control over. It does not mean that your marketing materials are bad.

7. Are you submitting for projects that are out of your reach? Are you trying to get the lead in a studio film where they are looking for "name" talent? If the project is out of your reach at this point in your career, then you are likely to not be called in unless they've seen hundreds of people and still have not met the person that is a match for the character they are casting.

8. Are you looking in the right places for auditions? Are you just using *Backstage*? Are you just using one website to look for auditions? Then

perhaps you should expand the places that you check for auditions. Every website does not have the same auditions on it, so again, be a detective and find out which site has the opportunities you want.

9. When opportunity knocks will you be ready? How are your auditioning skills? Are they rusty? If they are, then take a class to brush up your skills. Have you been getting callbacks when you have auditions? If not, then seriously consider taking an audition class or a class that focuses on a specific set of auditions skills. Auditioning for a film requires a different set of skills than auditioning for a commercial or for the theatre. Develop the auditioning muscles that allow you to successfully audition for any medium.

10. Does your current look support what you are selling? Is your hairstyle the same one that is currently in your headshot? If you dye your hair another color, are your roots showing? Are you dressing appropriately for your auditions? If you've been called in for the role of a Wall Street banker, are you showing up to the audition in torn jeans and a T-shirt? If you've been called in to audition for role of a professional, dress like one. Have you gained or lost weight since you took your pictures? Personal appearance and hygiene is part of being in this business. You may be auditioning for the role of a street person, but you don't need to smell like one. Be aware of strong perfumes and colognes. Be conscious that the person that you are auditioning for may have allergies and because of that, will be focusing on your perfume or cologne and not your performance.

11. ARE YOU HAVING FUN? If you haven't found a way to make your marketing fun for you and have started to dread the audition process, it will show. Do you need an attitude adjustment? Perhaps it's time to reconnect to your passion for acting. Maybe it is time to take a class that will help you recharge your batteries.

12. Are you being safe? Is there a phone call you are putting off making? Is there a letter you want to write, but can't seem to find the time or energy to do it? Are you unhappy with the agent you do have and are simply grumbling about how she or he is treating you, instead of going in and having a conversation to clear the air? Is it time for you to stop doing student films and theatre that takes place in coffeehouses and time for you to move toward joining one of the unions and stepping up professionally? At some point, you need to face your fear about what's next for you as an actor and start making "what's next" happen. If you find that you are playing it safe, this is a time to check in with your support network and accountability group. You don't have to go it alone. The only

thing you have to do is make the decision that you want to take a bold action in your career. Then, after you make the decision, you connect with your community to find the support you need to do it. Invite people you trust to help you brainstorm next steps and then to hold you accountable for doing what you say you want to do.

If, after examining any of the previous areas, you haven't broken through your "dry spell," try this career assessment exercise. Mark off which ones are true for you (and yes, you can have half points):

Career Evaluation Form

_____ I enjoy auditioning.

_____ I am confident in my auditioning skills.

_____ I am confident in my craft as an actor and acting technique.

_____ I take at least five actions per week to create audition or acting opportunities for myself.

_____ I market myself consistently.

_____ I have pictures and a resumé that I love and that represents me perfectly.

_____ I have marketing materials that help support a professional image (postcards, cover letters, etc.).

_____ I have a record-keeping system for auditions and know the names of whom I audition for and when I've auditioned for them.

_____ I stay in contact with people I've auditioned for and/or who can help me in my career (mailings and follow-up).

_____ I have a plan for achieving my dreams and goals.

_____ I have found a way to handle the ups and downs and frustrations that occur in my career.

_____ I have a full and satisfying life outside of my work as an actor. My work and personal life are in balance.

_____ I have fun with my art and find ways to be creative for the joy of it.

_____ I network and either have or am building relationships with people that can help me move my career forward.

_____ I have a professional network I can tap into when I need information. (a good monologue coach, a class, information on good casting websites, etc.).

_____ I have money put aside for acting expenses and my acting business.

_____ I'm knowledgeable about casting directors, agents, and projects currently being cast.

_____ I see or am familiar with plays, films, television shows, music, and commercials that I can be cast in and am able to discuss why I am a good match for those roles.

_____ I have made peace with the idea that I'm selling a product—me.

_____ I know where to research for info I need on a play, film, director, casting director, etc.

_____ I have a direct and winning answer to: "Tell me about yourself."

_____ I can concisely tell people what I do in a way that interests them.

_____ I know what makes me unique as a performer and what only I can do as an actor (positioning statement/brand).

_____ I am able to be myself with agents, casting directors, directors, producers, writers, and other actors. I keep my acting skills where they belong: onstage or in front of the camera.

_____ I know how to create my own opportunities.

_____ **Total (of a possible 25)**

If you marked off all of the 25 items on the list as true, congratulations!

But, rarely, can anyone mark off all 25 as true. And, let's get honest, if you could mark off all 25 as true, you wouldn't be reading this book.

So, consider taking one of the items and focusing your energy and efforts on making it true for you. For example, do you find yourself getting frustrated with the ebb and flow of auditions and opportunities in your career? Here are a few ways for you to handle this frustration:

1. Watch a good movie; go see good theatre. Reconnect to your dream by watching something that inspires you.

2. Take a nonacting related class or workshop. Try an art class. Try belly dancing. Try kickboxing. The idea here is challenge yourself or your creativity in a new way.

3. Have fun. Yes, this is a simple suggestion. You can get so focused on your goal that you lose perspective. A good laugh is good for your outlook and health.

4. Indulge yourself. Have a massage. Spend some money on you. Pamper yourself.

5. Make an accomplishment list for yourself. Yes, you would like to be further along in your career, but don't forget to take the time to acknowledge what you have achieved so far.

So, take one of the 25 items that you did not mark as true and brainstorm a list of actions that can help you change it from false to true.

_____

_____

_____

_____

_____

_____

_____

_____

_____

_____

_____

_____

_____

_____

_____

_____

_____

_____

_____

_____

_____

_____

_____

_____

_____

_____

_____

_____

_____

_____

_____

_____

_____

_____

Another approach you can use when you are experiencing a dry spell is to reassess your original goal. **Is the goal you selected in Chapter 5 the right goal for you?** Sometimes we select a goal because it is sensible and not because it excites us. If working in movies is what you really want to do, why are you wasting your valuable time on trying to get started as a commercial actor? Wouldn't a better goal for you be working toward booking a great part in a quality film production?

Think about it. If you've structured your goal as: If I do _____ (fill in the blank), then I can get to have _____ (fill in the blank). If I go out and do stand-up comedy, then I'll get a sitcom. Yes, this is one way to reach the goal, but not everyone gets offered a development deal because they do stand-up. You do stand-up because you love to do stand-up and being offered a development deal comes out of your joy for comedy. And, there are actors who do get sitcoms without doing stand-up. Ray Romano is a stand-up comedian and the star of his sitcom, the actor who played his brother is also a stand-up comedian—and the other three principal performers aren't. Wouldn't it make more sense to focus on the main goal? Don't misunderstand. You can have a commercial career, you can have a theatre career, and a movie career all at the same time. But when you start out, it makes more sense to focus on getting started in the area that excites you, so that you actually take the marketing actions to make it happen.

Another approach to breaking through a dry spell is to **create your own opportunities.** What about taking a writing class and writing a script? What about taking the script and making your own movie, with you as the star of it? There are a number of websites where you can post your work online. Episodic shows (for example, online soap operas) are being shot and shown every week on the web. How about producing your own play? If you don't want to write, there are plenty of writers who would love to see their work produced. The key points here are to find a way to channel your creativity and find a way to BE SEEN. Remember, the more you work the more your confidence as a performer will grow. And, once again, work breeds work. There is an old saying which says it is easier to look for a new job when you have one. This saying applies to actors as well. So, consider organizing your own production—it can lead to work as well as help you break through your dry spell.

Maybe you are one of the lucky actors whose marketing efforts are getting you **auditions,** but the dry spell you are experiencing is that you **aren't booking the roles.** Even though you aren't booking work you can still feel like every audition you attend is a success. You can make every audition you attend a success by learning to separate the things you can control from those you can't.

What you can't control: The casting director wants to hire his third cousin twice removed and no matter how great your audition is, you won't get the part. The financing broke down and the production is put on hold. They found this out the minute before you walked into the audition room. The scowls you saw on everyone's face had nothing to do with you! They've just invested months of their lives into a project that isn't going to happen and nothing you do will change their minds or improve their moods. You remind someone of their ex-husband/boyfriend or ex-wife/girlfriend and they had a really ugly divorce/break-up. No matter how wonderful and talented you are, you won't get that job. The schedule of a major name actor opened up and s/he wants YOUR part. Even if you gave the audition of a lifetime, you won't get the role because of reasons you have no control over!

What you can control:

- Being prepared professionally and as an artist
- Creating business standards for yourself
- Defining what success looks like to you
- Creating an audition/victory log

Auditions are a way of life for the performing artist. Given that there are so many variables an actor has no control over, why not invest your energy in areas where your actions can make an impact?

Being prepared means getting a copy of the script or text before the audition if at all possible. It means doing your homework before you stand up to perform in an audition. Did you make strong choices with the material? Do you know the text so well that you can spend your time in the audition acting instead of having your face in the copy? How about getting your material coached before a big audition? Wouldn't that help you feel better prepared for the audition? If you can't afford a coach, what about working with other actors to get a better handle on the material? Being prepared as an artist means keeping your instrument tuned.

What does being prepared mean to you? What does it specifically look like to you? If you know that you have done the best job you can possibly do at an audition, then the results are secondary. You've done your best work. What does it take for you to do your BEST work?

Creating business standards means that you have ground rules for yourself as a professional. Can people trust you? Do you show up on time for auditions? Can you be counted on to show up when and where you need to? Do you keep your word?

Have you asked all the questions you need to when you get the audition? Who am I auditioning for? Where do I need to be? What time do I need to be there? What's the project? When is it shooting? Will you be available the days it's shooting if you are booked for the job?

Define what a successful audition is to you. Booking a job is a definite sign of success, but not every audition leads to a job. Decide what success looks like to you. When you have a personal definition of success, you don't have to wait for anyone to say you did well because you can measure your work against your personal standards.

For example, were you emotionally available during the audition? Did you remember to listen and interact with your scene partner during the audition? Were you alive through the whole scene, not just on your lines? Did you take direction easily? Did your nerves get the best of you during the audition? And, most importantly, did you remember to have FUN?

What would make an audition successful for YOU? Before you go to an audition, decide in advance what would make it successful. It can be as simple as getting through a new monologue for the first time. In this instance, if you get through the monologue, then the audition is a success no matter what.

Creating an audition/victory log will give you a record of your experiences at auditions. You can record whom you've met, what you performed, and how the audition went. It is a physical record of the actual audition, but it is also a tool for learning. Are you unhappy with the audition? Put your thoughts in your log. What starts to happen when you use this kind of tool is that you may begin noticing patterns about your work. It will help you develop a knowledge of the specifics that contribute to your being successful in an audition. Once you know what needs to be in place for you to succeed, you can then replicate this way of working each time you audition.

It is important to keep a victory log because there will be days when you need to read about your victories, for example, during one of your dry spells. Having a victory log is a great record that reminds you of your successes and victories. You can record favorable comments in your log. You can record bookings in your log. You can record callbacks. Anytime you receive praise for your work, record it! A victory log is a great way to remember the successes and accomplishments you experience on your journey as an actor or actress.

Set up an audition/victory log for yourself. Use your creativity to create a system that works for you. Some people use a beautiful notebook to write their thoughts and information in. Other people simply use a calendar. Find a system that you are comfortable with and use it.

The key to successful auditions is recognizing what you can and cannot control. As a performing artist, you spend so much time auditioning, instead of wondering if you are what the auditors are looking for or if they like you—focus your energy on finding specific and measurable ways to succeed on YOUR TERMS.

Although, we have discussed in previous chapters that acting is not a linear business, there is, however, a structure to the work cycle. Based on working actors and experiencing it professionally as well, here is a framework of how the process of working as an actor moves from start to finish.

First, you hear about the potential job. You hear about it through word of mouth (friends, your accountability group, an acting classmate) or you find out about it reading the trades or you see something on the various casting websites. The first step is that you learn of a potential job or a role that you know is a good match for your type and skills.

Then you put your picture and resumé AND a cover letter in the mail asking about the project or asking for an audition. In the cover letter you stress that you are excited about the project and feel that you can bring a unique interpretation to the work, and, you ask for an opportunity to audition for this great project.

Then you follow up. Make a phone call. Ask around your community—has casting started? Is there some action you can take to be seen for the project?

If you are right for the project, you'll get a call. Remember, when you get a call inviting you to attend, ask: Where is the audition? When is the audition? Is there any information on the character you can get? A little back story? Is there a special clothing requirement for the character? Can you get the sides and/or the entire script prior to the audition? If so, how soon can you get them? (FYI: Sides are what scenes are called when you audition for film and television. When you audition for commercials it is called "copy." Learn the language of your industry.) What kind of project is it? (Film, television, soaps, etc.—remember each medium requires a different acting skill set.) Do they want to see a monologue? Is the audition going to be on camera?

Once you get all the preliminary information, find the time to prepare for the audition. Work on the material. Never, ever, ever go in to an audition unprepared. It will show. You think you may be fooling the auditors, but it rarely happens that you'll get away with it.

You'll then attend the audition. After the audition, remember to write a thank-you note. You'll then work. After the job, remember to add the names of people on set who can potentially give you future opportunities to your database/tracking system. Follow up in 6 to 8 weeks with an update if you have something new to report (for example: new class, callback, booking, roles that you are working). When it comes to the updates, don't just drop a note in the mail that says: "I'm writing to say hi." It isn't professional. Say "hi" by giving an update on the work you've been doing professionally. Stay in contact with the people you've worked with. It is easier to be hired by someone who knows you and the quality of your work, than being hired by someone who is taking a chance on you for the very first time.

So, if you are having a dry spell in your career—is there an area in the work cycle you've overlooked? Is there a breakdown in this process? If there is, then focus your attention on building a bridge between one phase of the cycle and the next.

In every business people experience burnout. It is a given when it comes to work. There are times you love what you are doing and there are times when you don't. First, remember why you want to act and reconnect to that passion and then look around and see what actions you can take to recharge your batteries. Don't lose sight of what you want for yourself and in your career. Try to look at any dry spell you may experience from a new perspective, and keep working toward your dream of working as an actor.

Appendix

APPENDIX

Resource List

This section is devoted to helping you learn about and purchase resources that can help you find answers to the questions you have. There are hundreds of reference books and websites available to you. You could easily go into overwhelm mode trying to figure out what reference material is a good investment for your money. The resources below are what we recommend to our students in our classes and are a good place to start as you begin working on your business.

Please note: Information changes, trends come and go in this business—the books, websites, and the information suggested below are merely guideposts to help you get started on your journey as an actor.

New York

- *Henderson's Casting Director Guide* written by Sue Henderson. Sue has been publishing her CD book for a long time. She is very thorough with the information she provides. *www.hendersonenterprises.com*
- *The Ross Reports.* You can get the *Ross Reports* at any newsstand in New York and Los Angeles. You can also buy it online. The *Ross Reports* contain a listing of casting directors and agents for NY and LA. They also have a directory called the *USA Talent Directory* with listings for every state and Canada. The report comes out every month; we believe it is not necessary to purchase a new report every month. The information does not change that frequently. It is, however, a good idea to purchase a report every couple of months to stay current on any changes that happen in your professional community. You can purchase the *Ross Reports* online at *www.backstage.com.*
- *Backstage.* This newspaper is published once a week and is available on most newsstands. You can also get a subscription. The paper has articles and a listing of auditions in the New York area. *Backstage West* covers the West Coast with articles and a listing of auditions in LA. *www.backstage.com*

- *Theatrical Index.* Published weekly by Price Berkley. This is a listing of upcoming theatre productions in New York.
- *Show Business Weekly.* This is a weekly newspaper available at all newsstands in Manhattan. You can also find auditions at their website: *www.showbusinessweekly.com.*
- *The New York Agent Book* by K. Callan. She is also the author of *The L.A. Agent Book.* We LOVE these books and highly recommend them. The books are fun to read and are filled with great information. The first half of the book contains information on how to get an agent and then looks at how to deal with an agent after you've inked with him/her. The second half of the book gives a bio for every agent in NY. She follows the same format in her LA book. She also writes some interesting books that deal with life as an actor. You can find out more about her and her books at *www.swedenpress.com.*

Los Angeles

- *The Hollywood Reporter.* This is a daily paper that is filled with pertinent industry news, development deals, and projects in preproduction and currently in production. This is a good publication to read wherever you live because the information is targeted specifically to the entertainment industry. *www.thehollywoodreporter.com*
- *Variety.* Also a daily industry paper. Think of *Variety* as the *Wall Street Journal* for the entertainment industry. It is filled with facts and figures. *www.variety.com*
- *The Casting Director Guide* by Now Casting. This casting director guide is the only guide in LA that publishes the names of assistants as well as the main casting director; very thorough book. *www.nowcasting.com*
- *Ross Reports.* See NY listings for information.
- *The Los Angeles Agent Book* by K. Callan. See NY listing for more information.
- *Backstage West.* See NY listing for more information.

Other States and Canada

- *USA Talent Directory* published by Ross Reports. See NY listing.
- *The Season Overview.* A frequently updated listing of the major Regional Theatres in the USA and is available only at The Drama Bookshop.
- *Regional Theatre Directory.* Published annually by Theatre Directories at *www.theatredirectories.com.*

Other Helpful Books

- *Acting as a Business* by Brian O'Neil
- *Audition* by Michael Shurtleff. This book has been around for over 20 years and is still one of the premiere books on how to craft strong auditions.
- *How to Get the Part Without Falling Apart* by Margie Haber
- *Acting in Commercials* by Joan See
- *How to Audition for TV Commercials: From the Ad Agency Point of View* by W. Jenkins. What makes this book interesting is that he looks at the commercial casting process from the point of view of the advertising agency.
- *American Theatre Magazine*. Published 10 times annually by Theatre Communications Group. *www.tcg.org*
- *How to Sell Yourself as an Actor: From New York to Los Angeles and Everywhere in Between* by K. Callan
- *Auditioning and Acting for the Camera* by John W. Shepard. This is a great book that takes you through auditioning for every type of job available to an actor and what is expected of you. He discusses soap operas, commercials, episodic TV, feature films, and more.
- *The Fan Club Game* by Jay Perry. *www.playthegameof.com*
- *Action! Professional Acting for Film and Television* by Robert Benedetti
- *Acting: Advanced Techniques* by Terry Schreiber. Terry's work originates from The Method. He has been teaching and directing for over 36 years and has developed his own unique approach to help actors create truthful performances.
- *Your Film Acting Career: How to Break into the Movies & TV & Survive in Hollywood* by M. K. Lewis and Rosemary R. Lewis

You can purchase many of the above books at Amazon, Barnes and Noble, or Borders.

Other great book purchasing resources are used book websites. Check out *www.alibris.com* or *www.housingworksbookstore.org*. At the Housing Works site, 100% of the profits go to the Housing Works in NYC. Housing Works is a nonprofit organization that provides healthcare, job training, advocacy, and housing to the homeless in NYC.

When purchasing any of the books listed, make sure you are getting the most recent edition in publication.

Bookstores and Websites

The Drama Book Shop, Inc.
250 W. 40th St.
New York, NY 10018
Tel: (212) 944-0595
www.dramabookshop.com

Samuel French Bookstore
11963 Ventura Blvd.
Studio City, CA 91604
Tel: (818) 762-0535

7623 Sunset Blvd.
Hollywood, CA 90046
Tel: (323) 876-0570
www.samuelfrench.com

Websites with useful articles and information:
http://actingbiz.com/articles/
http://more.showfax.com/columns.php
www.imdb.com Want to find out what movies an actor has done, go to this
  website. Want to find the synopsis of a movie, go to this website. This is
  a useful website for you as you start to do your branding work and are
  looking researching characters that the actors have portrayed.
Websites with auditions and places to post your headshot and resumé:
www.backstage.com
www.craigslist.com (Please exercise caution with some of the audition
  notices on this website. Always make sure you audition in a public
  place. Do not go to anyone's apartment to audition.)
www.actorsaccess.com
www.lacasting.com
www.nycasting.com
www.mandy.com You'll find some good auditions here; again, exercise
  caution.
www.nyc.gov/html/film/html/locations/current_nyc_productions.shtml
This website tells you what projects are in production in NYC.

Classes

Finding the right acting or singing coach is a very personal choice. Once or twice a year, *Backstage* puts out a coaches and acting classes issue in New York and LA. Make a list of what you want to achieve in acting class or with a vocal coach and go shopping for a coach that meets your needs and goals. Word of mouth is also a great way to connect with a coach. Ask for references from your acting friends. If you are pursuing an acting career outside of New York or LA, check out the local professional theatre for names of coaches and acting classes.

Makeup and Clothing

You can purchase makeup and learn how to apply makeup for the camera at any makeup counter in a department store. MAC and Sephora are two popular makeup brands. The Make-Up Center in NYC specializes in working with actors and has been in business for a long time. Please note that the application of street makeup is completely different than theatrical makeup, which is completely different than on-camera makeup. Learn what is acceptable in the medium you will be working.

For clothes, first make a list of the clothing you will need for audition purposes. For example, a long black skirt for Shakespeare and classical auditions. For guys, consider purchasing a loose-fitting, flowing shirt or something with a high collar. Think of clothing that will give the impression of clothing from another time and era. With regard to contemporary audition clothing, find clothing that is flattering to you and on your body.

Colorful clothes look good on camera. Stay away from heavily patterned shirts because they cause feedback on camera, stay away from white because white reflects light, stay away from black clothing because it absorbs light, and stay away from red for videotaping because red tends to bleed. So, what does that leave you—blues, purples, rust, greens, and every other color in the spectrum. Also, please stay away from big earrings in an audition. Because you are being taped in a medium frame (about the second button on a shirt with buttons), they tend to reflect light and the viewer tends to focus on them and not you. Also, for the same reason, stay away from logos on your clothing. Again, the viewer focuses on the logo and not you because the logo becomes the most important visual in the frame.

There are some great discount places in New York and almost every city in the United States. In New York check out Filene's Basement, Daffy's,

Century 21, Target, K-Mart, and the many second-hand shops where you can find designer clothing at a fraction of the original price. You can find what you need without spending a fortune.

Supplies

For office supplies, check out Office Depot or Staples. Consider purchasing an inexpensive fax machine so that you can send off your resumé with ease and also receive your sides as soon as possible prior to an audition.

You'll also find vendors in *Backstage* that will print up your resumé in bulk for you. Kinko's is another good option for printing your resumé.

NOTES